The Tennis Book

The Tennis Book

A Young Player's Guide to Tennis

Tom and Gillian Kern

KEY PORTER BOOKS

National Library of Canada Cataloguing in Publication Data

Kern, Tom
The tennis book : a young player's guide to tennis / Tom and Gillian Kern.

Includes index.
ISBN 1-55263-235-0

1. Tennis—Juvenile literature. I. Kern, Gillian II. Title.

GV996.5.K47 2003 j796.342 C2003-905175-7

The Canada Council for the Arts since 1957 | Le Conseil des Arts du Canada depuis 1957

Ontario Arts Council
Conseil des Arts de l'Ontario

The publisher gratefully acknowledges the support of the Canada Council for the Arts and the Ontario Arts Council for its publishing program.

We acknowledge the financial support of the Government of Canada through the Book Publishing Industry Development Program (BPIDP) for our publishing activities.

We acknowledge the support of the Government of Ontario through the Ontario Media Development Corporation's Ontario Book Initiative.

Key Porter Books Limited
70 The Esplanade
Toronto, Ontario
Canada M5E 1R2

www.keyporter.com

Design: Peter Maher
Electronic formatting: Jean Lightfoot Peters
Photography: Jay Gundu
Illustrations: John Lightfoot

Printed and bound in Hong Kong, China

04 05 06 07 08 5 4 3 2 1

To my mom & dad, for instilling in me a love of games, and to Dudley Bell, for taking a chance on me.
TOM KERN

To my parents, who provided me with the opportunities to play sports, and to my boys, who inspire me to continue.
GILLIAN KERN

Contents

Acknowledgments 8

Foreword 9

To the Parents 10

Introduction 12

1/Equipment 18

2/Getting Started 26

3/Playing the Game 40

4/Specialty Shots 62

5/Strategy and Tactics 72

6/Doubles 80

7/Rules 86

8/Etiquette 94

9/Tournaments 98

10/Nutrition—Eat to Compete! 102

Talking Tennis 107

Tennis Resources 110

Index 111

Key to Symbols:

Trivia

Technical

Experiment

Rule Book

Tactics

Drill

Acknowledgments

Thank you to friends and family for support, Leaside Tennis Club for access to the courts, The Merchant of Tennis for supplying props, the Dea family for the laptop, Peter Cameron and Ari Novick for advice and, of course, our wonderful junior players: Kai, Liam, Alexandra, Ethan, Elizabeth and Sean. A special thank you to Jag Gundu for the fabulous photos.

Foreword

When I was three years old, my Mom and Dad leashed me to the net post while they played tennis with each other. Tennis has been a big part of my life ever since!

I played against the wall on my porch until the noise drove my parents crazy. I played in parks, at schools and at tennis clubs throughout my childhood. I tried out for my high school tennis team, but didn't make it. Never one to give up, I tried out again in college, and this time the coach saw some potential.

After twenty-four years of teaching tennis, I am now extremely proud to be called "Coach" by students young and old. Tennis is awesome! I hope that on these pages you'll find the fun and excitement that I discovered with tennis in my life. So turn the page and let's get going!

—Tom Kern

Coach Tom in action

To the Parents

Whether or not you play tennis, the fact that you are looking at this book indicates you are aware that tennis is a sport that can enhance your child's life.

Apart from the obvious physical fitness benefits of playing a sport regularly, tennis offers your child more intangible benefits, including life skills such as fair play, etiquette and determination, not to mention fun!

This book takes an interactive approach to learning tennis. With "hands on" instruction, we take your child through an introduction to the sport, getting comfortable with the ball and racket on your driveway or in the schoolyard, to playing a regular game of tennis on a proper tennis court. Tactics and strategies are covered, along with rules, nutrition tips and information on professional tennis. We have included an appendix with a list of resources so that your child may contact clubs or organizations in your area to follow up with lessons or competitive opportunities.

Of course, children (and adults) learn best when they are entertained. You'll find lots of trivia, tidbits and statistics to keep your child interested and amused. Because you are supporting your child in this venture, there is an even greater chance of success. Your support can take many forms: you can give your child this book, read it together and practice or play with your child. You might also consider finding a tennis professional to assist your child.

Whichever you choose, you are giving your child a lifelong gift, so go ahead...
"Try, learn, play!"

P.S. This book should be of interest to the young at heart as well as the young in years. Enjoy!

Patrick Rafter

Introduction

Tennis is a sport played all over the world. It is played by presidents, princesses and movie stars. Right now there are children learning tennis in Japan, Mexico and Tunisia. There are courts, leagues and tournaments in more than 140 countries, and tennis is an official medal sport in the Summer Olympics.

But it all starts right here, in your neighborhood. All you need is a ball and a racket. You can learn a lot about tennis on your own, hitting against a wall, on your driveway or at your school, developing the skills necessary to play the greatest game in the world.

Jelena Dokic

THE HIGH BORNE PRINCE IAMES DVKE OF YORKE.
borne October = the 13. 1633.

No one knows where the name "tennis" came from. Some think that it may have come from the French word "tenez," meaning "take it." Others believe it was named after one of two towns. There is a town in France called "Tennis" and also one in Egypt. We may never know for sure where the name came from.

Tennis got its start with a ball and a wall about seven hundred years ago in France (in the thirteenth century). Kings and queens in the royal court invented a game to play called "le jeu de paume," which means "the game of the palm." This French game had very complicated rules and was played on an indoor court by hand-hitting a ball against the walls and the roof of the court. Soon rackets were added, and the game evolved into one that is now called "court tennis." Court tennis is only played in a few places in the world today, but it was the predecessor to the very popular game of tennis.

About three hundred years after the game was invented, near the end of the sixteenth century, it spread to England. In 1874, a man named Major Walter Clopton Wingfield decided to combine the most exciting elements of court tennis with a few other games (namely, cricket, croquet and badminton), to come up with a game called Sphairistike, which comes from the Greek word for "play." Major Wingfield's game was played outdoors on a grass court because he thought it would make the game seem more "elegant." He also figured he could earn lots of money by selling expensive equipment for his new game.

The All England Croquet Club liked the idea of the new game, and in 1876, they adapted Major Wingfield's game again, changing the height of the net and the shape of the court (from an hourglass shape to a rectangle). The first lawn tennis championships were

Sphairistike

played at the newly named All England Croquet and Lawn Tennis Club in 1877. The game of tennis has changed very little since then.

Like all great games, the popularity of tennis began to spread. In North America the game really caught on, and grass courts were built in Staten Island, New York, and Toronto, Ontario. In 1881 the first U.S. national tournament was organized by Dr. James Dwight, a man who is now known as "The Father of American Tennis." The game of tennis continued to grow quickly in popularity after the tournament, in both Europe and North America.

The All England Croquet and Lawn Tennis Club is much too long a name. Most people just call it "Wimbledon" after the part of London where the club is located.

While the game kept evolving—with some rule changes and the addition of different court surfaces—the height of the net and the shape of the court have stayed the same since the original All England tournament in 1877.

Until 1968 competitive tennis was played by "amateurs" (players who did not get paid). Sometimes the top players would go on tour and people would pay money to see them play. These players were called "professionals" because they earned money for playing tennis. Getting paid meant that they were excluded from playing amateur tournaments such as Wimbledon and the United States championships.

Serena Williams

Finally, in 1968, officials in England and the United States decided that they wanted the best players in their tournaments, so they allowed professional players in to compete against the amateurs. They figured it would be more exciting and more profitable—and they were right. The players we see on television today are all professionals, and the very top men and women on the Pro Tour make millions of dollars per year!

Serena Williams, one of the top female American players, set a new women's record for prize money earned in a single season by winning $3,935,668.00 in 2002. She also makes millions of dollars by endorsing products for different companies. Her sister Venus is not far behind her!

Tennis is also played by wheelchair athletes. The rules are modified so that the ball may bounce twice before being hit.

The International Tennis Federation (ITF) is the world's governing body for tennis. The ITF is in charge of rules, officials, technical specifications and lots of other tennis business. More than one hundred countries belong to the ITF.

Did you know that a tennis court can be made of many different surfaces? The main ones are grass, asphalt and clay, but others include carpet, rubber and... cow dung! No kidding! Cow dung, dried and hardened, is an official surface on some courts in India.

1/Equipment

The basic equipment you'll need to play tennis is a racket and a ball. Of course, if you are a very enthusiastic player, there is a lot more equipment out there that can enhance your game. There are even stores dedicated to selling tennis equipment. The following pages will help you get started by telling you all you need to know about tennis equipment.

Arantxa Sanchez Vicario and Martina Navratilova

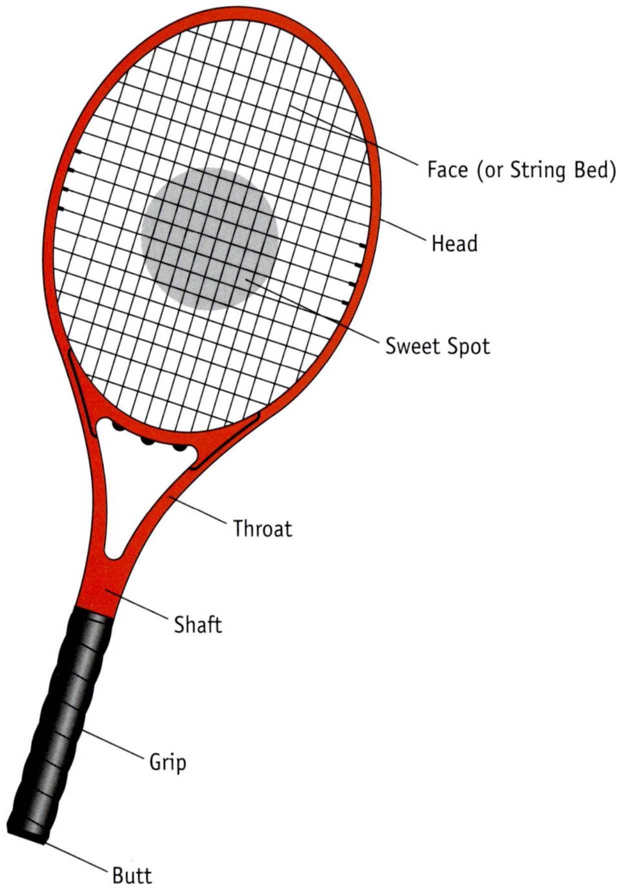

Diagram of racket

The maximum width of a tennis racket is 12.5 inches (31.75 cm) and the maximum length is 29 inches (73.5 cm). The string surface must not exceed 15.5 inches (39.5 cm) in overall length and 11.5 inches (29 cm) in overall width.

Rackets

Probably the biggest change in tennis has been the way rackets are constructed. Early tennis rackets were made of wood and weighed from 12 to 16 ounces (350 to 450 g). Today's rackets are constructed from materials like Kevlar, graphite and titanium and can weigh as little as 8 ounces (225 g). These lightweight, powerful rackets have enabled more people to play tennis, and have increased the popularity and competitiveness of the game.

There is a wide range of rackets available today, in all shapes and sizes. The development of junior rackets has enabled younger children to be successful on the court. Junior rackets are shorter and lighter than those for adults. There are four lengths available in junior rackets: 21, 23, 25 and 26 inches (53, 58, 64 and 66 cm). In addition, they are available in different weights ($6\frac{1}{2}$ to 9 ounces, or 185 to 255 g) and grip sizes (between 3 and 4 inches, or 8 and 10 cm). Junior rackets are recommended for beginners up to about the age of eleven. Once you become more skillful, you can move up to a regular adult racket. With adult rackets you have a choice of head size (regular, midsize, oversize and supersize). You can also buy stretch rackets, which are a little longer in length. Grip sizes for adult rackets range from $4\frac{1}{4}$ to $4\frac{5}{8}$ inches (10.7 to 10.9 centimeters) in circumference.

With such a wide variety of rackets available, you are sure to find a racket to suit your needs. A coach or a knowledgable salesperson at a tennis store can help you choose the right racket.

Old wooden rackets from the early twentieth century

Junior, regular and oversized rackets

Don't be fooled by the size of the racket's head. You still have to hit the ball in the middle of the strings (called the "sweet spot") to hit a quality shot. In fact, a bigger racket is often harder to control. The sweet spot is just below the absolute center of the strings (known as the center of percussion). It is the ideal spot for the ball to hit the strings.

Strings

Most strings are made of woven nylon, but sometimes you'll come across people who still use gut. Made from animal intestines, gut is the most expensive stringing material around. Many of the professional players really like the way it "plays," and, considering what they are paid, it's not as if they need to worry too much about the cost!

There are many different types of tennis balls.

Balls

Tennis balls can be any color, but the most common is yellow. The inside of a tennis ball is made of rubber, and the ball is covered with a mixture of wool and artificial fibers, like a carpet (this is called the nap). The size of a tennis ball is standard (about $2^{1}/_{2}$ inches, or 6.4 cm, in diameter), and the pressure inside the ball must be exact, so that when the ball is dropped from a height of 100 inches (255 cm) onto a concrete surface it will bounce to a height of 53 to 58 inches (135 to 147 cm).

Tennis balls usually come in a pressure-sealed tin, with three balls per tin. The pressurized tin keeps the balls fresh until you are ready to use them.

In professional tennis tournaments, six balls are used at a time. After the first seven games, the six balls are changed for six new ones, and then they are replaced again every nine games. This is done because tennis balls actually change shape and pressure from being hit so hard. Many tournaments keep new tins of balls in the refrigerator to help them maintain their perfect condition.

There are special tennis balls that are made for children who are using junior rackets. They are lighter and softer than regular balls, so they move more slowly. You will have more success early on with these special balls. They are available at most tennis stores.

Tennis balls can last a long time. Even when you find that they just aren't bouncing like they used to, you can still use them for street hockey, or to play "catch" with your dog. I've even seen tennis balls cut in half and put on the bottom of chair legs in a classroom to prevent the chair from scraping on the floor!

There are different tennis balls for different court surfaces. On soft courts, like clay, tennis balls tend to fluff up more, so soft court balls have a thinner nap to help prevent too much "fuzziness." On hard courts, balls will lose their nap, so hard court balls have a thicker nap to start with.

Shoes and Clothing

It's important to wear the right kind of shoes on a tennis court. You'll be running, changing directions and stopping and starting a lot. Tennis shoes are designed for this kind of activity and will help prevent injuries such as sprained ankles or bruised heels. You should also remember that shoes only work if they are laced up properly. Some clubs also have rules about the type of shoes you can wear, because the wrong shoes can mark or harm the court surface.

Loose, comfortable clothing and proper tennis shoes should be worn when playing tennis.

The clothes you wear for tennis should always be loose and comfortable. Shorts and a T-shirt are usually fine, although some traditional clubs have an all-white clothing rule and will not allow cutoff shorts or sleeveless shirts.

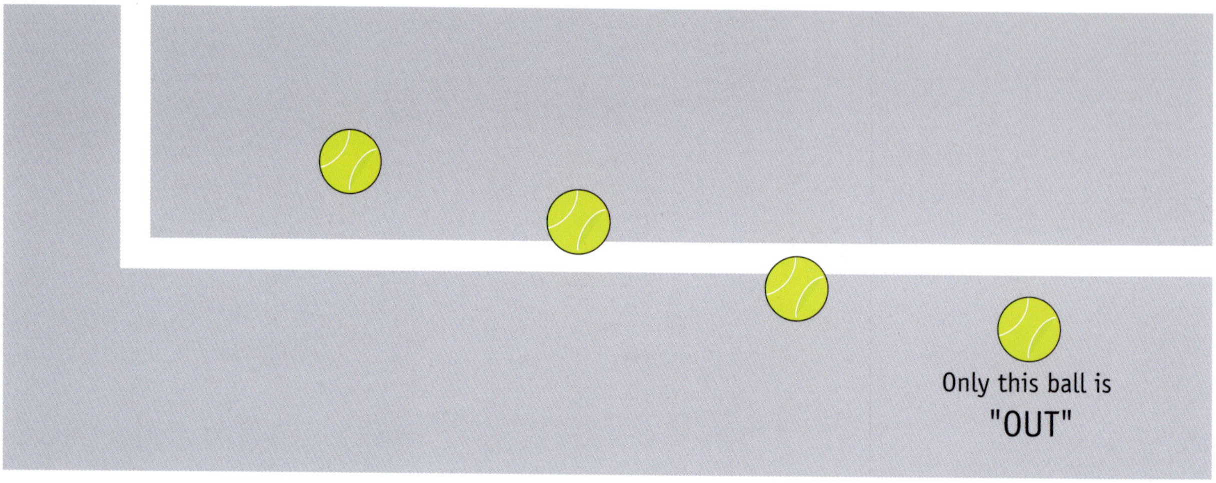

The lines are "good" in tennis. This means a ball that touches the line, even by just a fraction of an inch, is in.

It's usually a good idea to wear more than one layer of clothing so, as you warm up, you can take a layer off. The other thing to keep in mind is that you need big pockets to fit the tennis balls into. It is much easier to keep a couple of balls in your pocket, than to have to run and pick one up every time you miss. If you don't have pockets, a ball clip can do the trick. It clips onto your shorts or skirt and holds one ball.

The Court

You need a lot of space for an official tennis court. Including

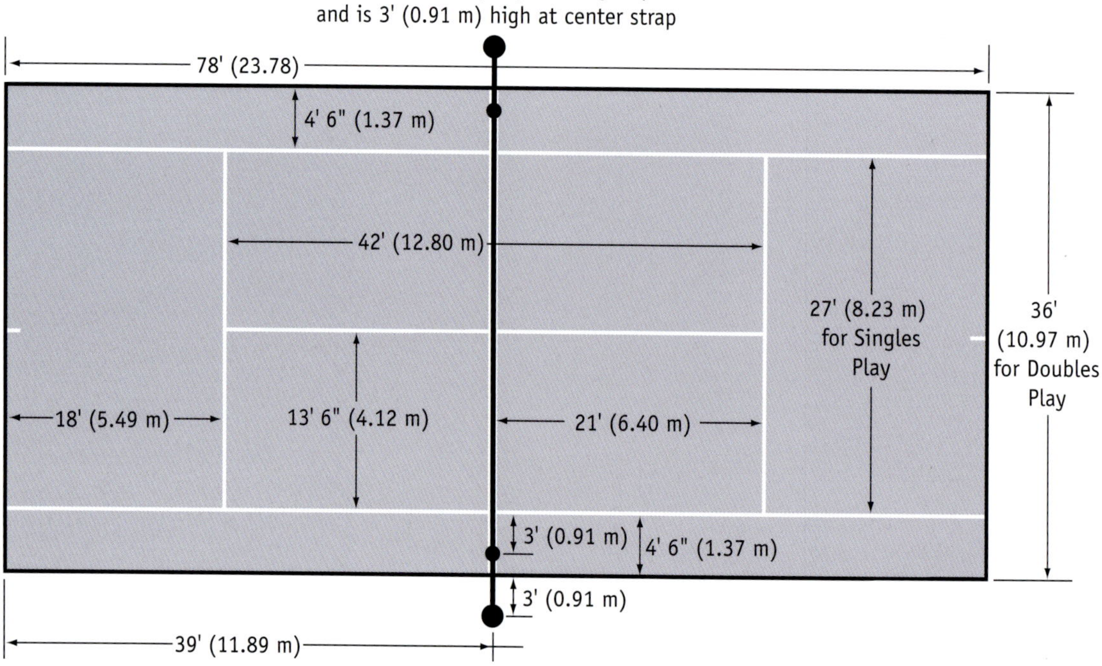

Tennis court measurements

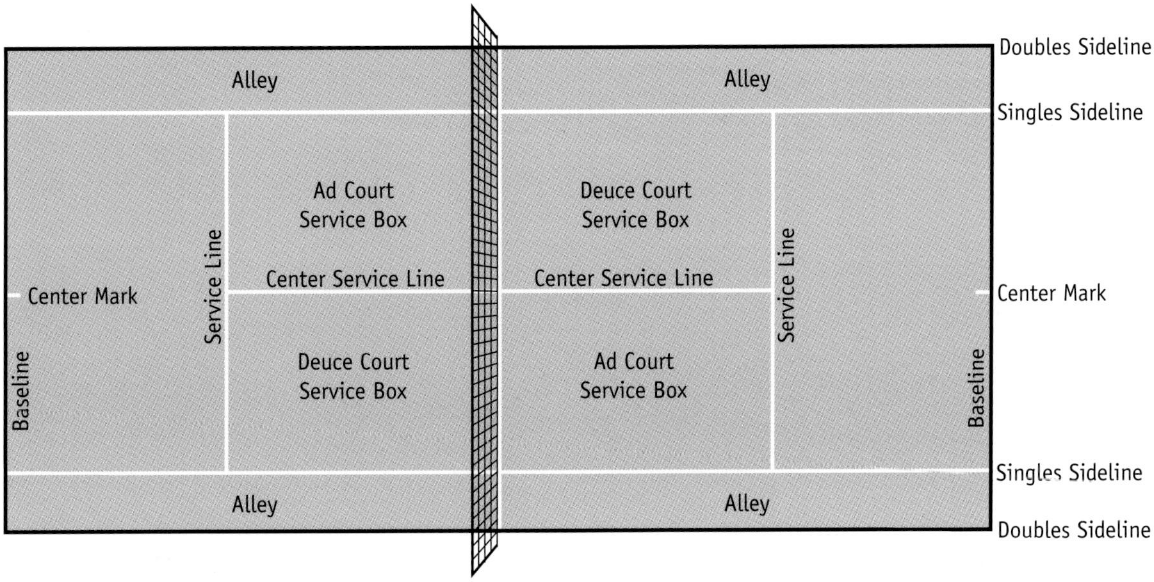

the space at the ends and to the sides of the court, you need an area of about 120 feet by 60 feet (36 m by 18 m). You could park a lot of cars on a space that size, or grow a lot of corn, so it is no wonder that tennis courts aren't in everyone's backyard. But the good news is that, in North America and Europe, just about every neighborhood has a court or two.

The nets are usually made of woven nylon, but some neighborhood courts use metal fencing for nets because it lasts a long time.

The net measures 3 feet (90 cm) high in the middle, but if you look closely, you'll notice that the sides of the net, near the net posts, are 6 inches (15 cm) higher. This is a good thing to keep in mind when you want to hit the ball over the net near the side. Aim high!

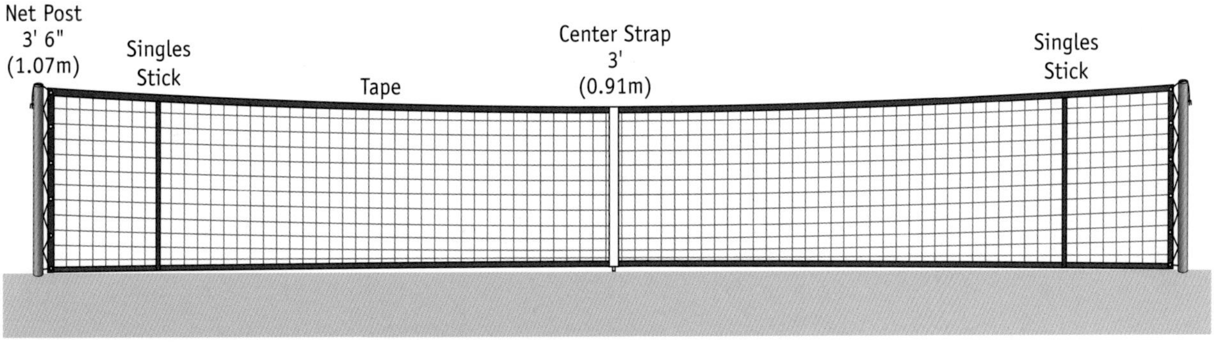

2/Getting Started

Now that you've got all your equipment straight, you are almost ready for action.

First, you need to figure out how to hit the ball over the net. If you can get it over one time more than your opponent, you'll win lots of matches. The following twelve steps will help you learn how to get the ball over the net. While you don't need a court or an opponent for the twelve steps, you'll still learn a lot of the skills necessary to play tennis. This way, when you finally do hit the courts, you'll be way ahead of the game!

Lleyton Hewitt

Skipping

Ankle rolls

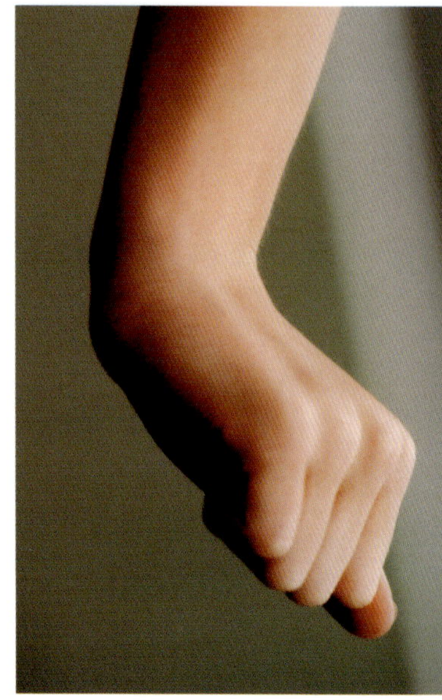

Wrist rolls

Step 1: The Warm-up

The most important piece of equipment that you need to get started is your body. Your muscles need to be fired up and ready for action. An easy way to warm up is by jogging slowly, skipping rope or riding your bike. This will help your heart pump blood through your body faster.

Next, is the ankle warm-up. Point one toe on the ground and make ten circles in each direction with your heel. Remember to do both feet. Wrist warm-ups should follow next. Make a fist and rotate your hands in ten circles, both ways.

Now you need to prepare your body to go fast. Most tennis points last less than ten seconds, so you need to be fast, in short bursts of speed. Take a thirty-second break between each of the next five exercises.

For the first exercise, run on the spot as fast as you can for five seconds. (This should make your whole body jiggle!) Next, run about ten steps forward, as fast as you can, then turn sideways and shuffle back to where you began. Make sure you pump your arms while running, even the arm that's holding the racket. Now stand beside a line or a mark on the ground. Jump sideways over the line, back and forth, as fast as you can, five times.

Jumping over a line

Warm-ups should always be done before every tennis session, or any other athletic activity.

High knees

Upper body warm-up

Ready for high knees? Hold your racket out in front of you. Jog in place, bringing your knees up to touch your racket. Continue for a count of five. Then kick your feet backwards, again for a count of five.

Now let's get your upper body moving. Hold onto the top and bottom of your racket. Bend your knees slightly, keep your eyes forward, and swing your racket from side to side, swinging as far as you can in either direction five times.

Once you finish these exercises, you should feel warm and ready to go!

Step 2: Making Friends with Your Racket

Now you need your racket. To make sure it is comfortable in your hand, put your racket on the ground in front of you and, using your dominant hand, spread your hand over the grip and pick up the racket. You can adjust your grip a little until it's comfortable.

With the palm of your racket hand facing up, put the ball on the racket face (the strings). If you are using the special softer balls this will be a bit easier. Roll the ball

Try rolling the ball in circles on your strings.

Try balancing the ball on your racket with your eyes closed and standing on one leg.

gently around on the racket face without dropping it. Notice how tightly you're gripping the racket and try to relax your hand. How many circles can you do? Try going in the other direction. Now try keeping the ball completely still in the middle of your racket face. Try holding the racket with both hands, remembering to keep your hands close together so that they just touch each other. Keep your dominant hand closest to the bottom of the grip.

Next, try walking around while balancing the ball on your racket. Can you keep the ball balanced if you are standing on one leg or with your eyes closed?

Now turn your hand over so that your palm is facing the ground and do it all again. The more you practice balancing the ball on your racket, the more comfortable and skillful you will be when you finally hit the court.

There are a few different ways to figure out which is your dominant hand. Usually, your dominant hand is the one you write with, eat with and throw with. Some people are lucky enough to be able to do all these things with either hand. Try the drills with both hands and see which feels best to you.

Practice rolling the ball on the ground. Use your racket to guide the ball in front of you.

Step 3: Rolling the Ball

Put the ball on the ground in front of you. Point your racket down to the ground and, with your palm facing away from you, push the ball around. Keep the ball in front of your body. Set up an obstacle course and try to move through it quickly, keeping control of the ball. Next, go through the obstacle course with your palm facing toward you like you are pushing the ball with the back of your hand. Now dribble the ball through the course using both sides of your racket. Playing street hockey with your racket is fun, and good for learning tennis, too, but not so good for your racket.

You'll notice that all the drills we give you are done both with your palm up and then with your palm down. It is important to be able to hit the ball on both sides of your body and these palm up and palm down drills will really help you later on when you're hitting forehands and backhands.

When practicing with your racket, it might help you to imagine that the face of your racket has eyes. The ball will always go in the direction that the eyes are facing, so when your strings touch the ball make sure the eyes of your racket are looking where you want the ball to go.

Step 4: Catching Frogs

Holding the racket in your dominant hand with your palm up, use your other hand to gently toss a ball up to eye level. Let the ball bounce in front of you and then try to catch it on your strings between your shoulders and waist. This area is what we call the "strike zone." (We'll be mentioning the "strike zone" often. It is the ideal area for your ball and racket to meet.) Pretend you are

Catching Frogs

Toss the ball up to eye level, then let it bounce.

Toss the ball again. This time, hold your racket with your palm down.

Then try to catch it on your strings, with your palm up.

Try to catch the ball when it is in the "strike zone": the area between your waist and shoulders.

catching a frog in a net. Once you've caught ten "frogs" in a row, turn your racket hand over and try it the other way (palm down). Try this with two hands on your grip as well (remember that your dominant hand goes on the bottom).

Now start with the ball on your racket, palm up. Use your racket to toss the ball up to eye level and again catch the "frog." Try it palm down too.

Make a target, bounce the ball, bend your knees and try to hit it up to eye level.

Step 5: Rallying with Yourself

It is time to start hitting the ball! It may sound weird, but when you hit a ball it is important to use your legs as well as your racket. Start by putting the ball on your strings (holding the racket palm up). With your feet spread comfortably apart, toss the ball in the air to eye level. Let it bounce, bend your knees and hit the ball back up to eye level. Let it bounce on the ground again, and repeat. The trick is to get the ball to bounce in the middle of your racket. You should feel that your legs are helping you to lift the ball back into the air. Don't worry, while it is hard at first, it becomes easier with practice.

To challenge yourself, draw a chalk circle on the ground in front of you and try to get the ball in the circle on each bounce. Once you can do this ten times in a row standing still, try walking around while doing it, then try running. After you can do all this, wipe the sweat off your brow and try it all again, this time holding the racket palm down.

You should also try these exercises holding the racket with two hands on the grip.

Now you are rallying.

Step 6: Keeping the Ball in the Air

Now you're ready for a real challenge, the volley. Bounce the ball up on your racket without letting it hit the

Rally is the word used in tennis to describe hitting the ball one time after another without missing.

ground. Start by bouncing the ball very gently up in the air, keeping the ball very close to your strings. As you get better, try to make the ball bounce higher off your racket each time. The higher it goes, the harder it is to hit the middle of the racket when it comes down. Test yourself by seeing how many hits you can get in a row. Repeat this drill with your palm down, and again with two hands on the grip. Next, try it while alternating palm up and palm down on each hit.

Once you get good at volleying, you can practice while you're walking, talking, skipping or running. The better you get at these drills, the easier it will be for you to play a game of tennis.

Step 7: The Wall

Being ready to "hit the wall" is a bit like graduation day for a tennis player. There should be a good wall at a nearby school or park if you don't have space on your driveway. Remember to avoid walls with lots of windows. Balls don't bounce very well off glass panes!

The first thing you need to do is to get comfortable with the wall. Practice throwing and catching against the wall without your racket. Stand about three steps away from the wall. Gently toss the ball underhand against the wall. Let it bounce in front of you and try to catch it in your "strike zone" (between your waist and shoulders). Take one step back and do it again. When you are ten steps away you should switch to an overhand throw.

Notice where the ball has to hit the wall and where it lands on the ground in front of you so that it arrives in your strike zone at a comfortable speed. This is the height and bounce that you should aim for when you start hitting the ball against the wall with your racket. Receiving the ball in your strike zone is the key to good rallying.

It's time to try out the wall with your racket. The great thing about a wall is that it never misses!

Start three steps from the wall again. Turn slightly sideways so that your free hand (the hand you don't hold your

Keep the ball in the air.

Catch the ball in your strike zone.

When you hit the ball against the wall with your palm up, you are hitting a forehand shot.

racket in) is closer to the wall. Just as you practiced earlier, toss the ball against the wall to about eye level. After it bounces, gently lift the ball up and toward the wall with your racket by turning your shoulders forward (the eyes of your racket will be looking up high at the wall). Remember to hit it *gently*. Try to get the ball to come off the wall so that it bounces in front of you in your strike zone, then hit it again. Once you can do this ten times continuously, you are ready to back up a few more steps. (You'll notice that you are hitting the ball with your racket palm up in this sideways position. This will develop into your forehand stroke.) The farther away from the wall you get, the higher or faster you will have to hit the ball. Experiment with height, speed and direction to see if you can get the ball to come back to you in your strike zone.

Step 8: The Other Side (a.k.a. the Backhand)

Now stand sideways with your racket hand closest to the wall. Again, toss the ball to eye level in front of you, let it bounce, then turn your shoulders forward and lift the ball toward the wall. (Again, the eyes of the racket should look up at the wall.) When the ball comes off the wall, let it bounce and hit it again. Keep the rally going for as long as possible. As you get more confident, move farther away from the wall. Try using two hands on the grip as well, and remember to keep your dominant hand near the bottom of the grip. This palm-down stroke will evolve into your backhand.

Don't forget: only back up when you can hit ten in a row.

Hitting with your palm down develops your backhand shot.

Step 9: The Ready Position

Notice how the balls don't always come back to the same spot? Sometimes they go a little to the right or left, high or low, fast or slow. Tennis players have to be ready for all these situations. So let's work on the ready position.

Facing the wall, hold your racket with both hands and point it toward the wall (like a Jedi Knight would hold a light saber). Put your feet a little more than shoulder width apart. Now it's time to learn the three bends: ankles, knees and waist.

Bend your ankles and knees slightly so that your weight is a little bit forward on the balls of your feet. Bend a little forward at your waist as well. Gently bounce up and down. You should feel pretty balanced and ready to go! Try pushing

The ready position—pose like you're a Jedi Knight.

off to your right and see how far you can jump, then try it to the left, as well. Get back into your ready position and run forward to the wall as fast as you can. Pump your arms like a sprinter as you run. See how quickly you can turn and run back. The ready position should make all of these movements easier and faster.

This is what a proper unit turn looks like.

Step 10: Receiving the Ball from the Ready Position

When you were rallying on the wall using either palm up or palm down, you were in a sideways position when you received the ball. This time, you should face the wall in the ready position with both hands on the racket. Now you're ready to receive the ball on both your forehand and backhand sides. In an actual game of tennis, the ball can come to you on either side, so you've got to be prepared.

From the ready position, toss the ball (at eye level) to your right side and quickly turn your hips and shoulders to the right. Both hands should now be on the right side of your body and your toes should be pointing to the right as well. This is called the unit turn. It will prepare your body to strike the ball. Use small shuffle steps to position yourself for a perfect strike zone. Make contact with the ball in your strike zone and send it up against the wall. As the ball is traveling toward the wall, quickly get back into the ready position. When the ball hits the wall you must quickly decide if it is going to come to your forehand side again, or to your backhand side. When you've decided, use the unit turn again to turn your body quickly to that side and prepare to hit the ball again. Try hitting the ball with just one hand on the racket and with two hands.

If you continuously repeat this, you will be rallying with the wall.

Remember the sequence of events: Get ready, turn, hit, get ready, turn, hit, get ready, turn, hit, get ready...you've got it!

Step 11: Hitting High Balls

It is important to get comfortable hitting balls that are up over your head. Later on when you learn to serve you'll want to be really good at this. For now, toss the ball gently over your head and hit it with your racket palm up. Try to make it hit the wall high enough that it comes back to your strike zone. Keep the rally going for as long as possible.

Challenge yourself by creating targets.

Step 12: Mixing It Up

Here's where you can get creative! With a piece of chalk, draw a "net" 3 feet (90 cm) high on the wall. Try to make the balls hit the wall above the net. Draw a target above the net and try to hit the target. Change the target height. Reach as high as you can, or get a tall person to help you draw a high target. Try hitting the ball using one hand on both sides and two hands on both sides. Move closer to the wall and hit the ball *before* it bounces. The closer you get to the wall the less time you'll have to get sideways. If you get really close you won't have to move sideways at all. This is called volleying against the wall.

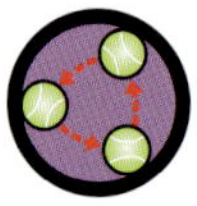

A fun way to challenge yourself to decide quickly is to call out "right" or "left" before the ball bounces on the ground. Try to get your body ready as soon as you've made your call.

The ready position is used in many sports.

If you can do all twelve steps, then you are ready to search out a nearby court. Keep practicing and make sure to do them all. The better you get at these twelve steps, the easier it will be for you once you do hit the court. If you have played a lot of other sports, you might master these twelve steps quickly.

When you make your racket face point up the ball goes higher, and when the face points to the wall the ball goes lower. The farther back you take your racket before you swing at the ball, the faster the ball goes. The only problem with that is, the faster the ball goes to the wall, the faster it comes back. It's easier when you hit the ball in front of your body. Experiment!

This ready position is used in many different sports. You might already be familiar with it from playing baseball (think of how an infielder stands), basketball (how do you move when you are guarding a player?) or football (look at the quarterback before the ball is snapped).

3/Playing the Game

If you are lucky, you will find a tennis court close to where you live. Next, you will need to find a partner to practice with. Get a brother, sister, mother, father, friend, neighbor or coach. Anyone will do, he just needs to be a good sport and want to have some fun. A good place to look for a partner is at your local tennis courts. Great minds think alike, and where there are tennis courts, there are tennis players!

Anna Kournikova

Mini-Tennis

The best way to start off on any tennis court is with both people close to the net, in a game called mini-tennis. Most professional players warm up this way, to help them get their rhythm and timing.

Mini-tennis is played in the service boxes using the singles sidelines. Start with a few co-operative drills, such as the Catch and Throw Drill on the right, and the Consistency Drill on the next page.

Once you're good at keeping a rally going, you can have a competition with your partner by playing a game of mini-tennis. In this game the server starts by standing behind the service line, on the right side of the center line. You serve into the service box that is diagonally opposite. You can serve the ball by bouncing it or by tossing the ball over your head and hitting it in an arc. If your first serve doesn't land in the box, you get one more chance. If both serves miss, your opponent wins the point.

If you get your serve in your opponent's service box, he

Catch and Throw Drill

Play mini-tennis without your racket. Throw the ball over the net in an arc. Your opponent has to catch it on one bounce. Then he throws it from where it was caught, and you must catch it after the bounce. Try to catch it in your strike zone. This is a great drill to help you learn to position yourself on the court to receive the ball well. (Try this drill with four people, too—it's really fun!)

Mini-tennis with two players

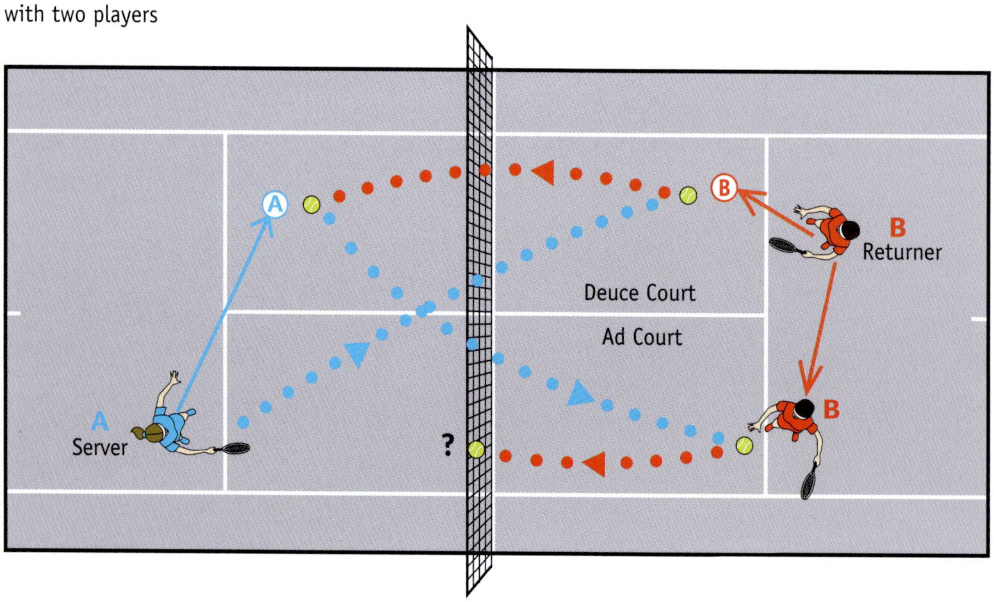

Player **A** vs Player **B**

A serves the ball by bouncing the ball and hitting it cross court into the deuce court service box.

B then has to get to the ball and, before it bounces twice, send it over the net into either service box.

A then has to retrieve that ball on one bounce and send it back to **B**. This continues until the ball bounces twice or is not returned into a service box.

The next point should be served into the ad court. Keep regular score or play one point at a time up to ten and alternate servers every five points.

This is the mini catch and throw drill in action.

must hit it back over the net after one bounce. The balls must land anywhere in front of the service line, between the singles sidelines. The last person to hit it over and in wins the point. The next point is started from the left side of the center line, again behind the service line, and again into the diagonally opposite service box. Switch servers after every five points. The game continues until someone wins ten points. Mini-tennis is a great way to get familiar with the movement and control that you need to keep the ball in play. Because the ball is moving a bit more slowly, it is easier to position yourself to hit the ball in your strike zone.

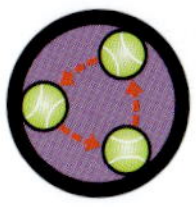

Consistency Drill
Using your rackets, rally as many balls as possible back and forth, keeping the bounce in front of the service lines. Notice that if you hit the ball in a low arc over the net you'll be able to have longer rallies. This should help you get more comfortable with the height, speed, direction and depth necessary to keep the ball in play.

Once you are pretty consistent with your mini-tennis game, you are ready to move back to the baseline.

At the Baseline

Wow...78 feet (24 m) from baseline to baseline! Do you feel like you need a pair of binoculars to see your partner? Don't panic. With all your work on the driveway, at the wall, and on the mini-tennis court, you've already learned a lot of the skills necessary to hit the ball from this distance.

Start by bouncing the ball and hitting it in an arc over the net. Watch your partner closely. Now's the time to make a few important observations. (Tennis players call this anticipation. It means making an educated guess about what

Try to meet the ball in the strike zone, between your waist and your shoulders.

your partner is going to do.) Is your partner running, reaching or off-balance? Is his back swing big or small? Do you think he will be able to hit the ball in front of his body or beside (or even behind)? Is he standing outside the sidelines, in the center of the court or deep behind the baseline? Where will he be able to send the ball from that location? All these clues will help you figure out what your partner may be able to do with the ball. The more you play, the better your anticipation skills will become. This gets more and more important as the level of your play (and of your opponent's) improves and the ball moves faster. Players with good anticipation skills rarely seem to be out of position.

Once you've taken your educated guess, you can then observe the ball in the air. Notice what happens when the ball is coming to you high over the net, lower over the net, faster and slower, close to the net or deep in the court. See if the ball has any spin on it. What happens then? These are the clues that will help you to position yourself to beat the ball to your strike zone.

Ready

Set

Go!

High/Low Drill *To train for speedy reactions, try this drill. Call out as soon as you see whether the oncoming ball is high over the net or low over the net. Try to call "high" or "low" as soon as you can after your opponent has hit the ball. Then move back to receive a high ball and forward to receive a low ball, so that you can hit the ball in your strike zone.*

Getting to the Ball

Okay you've anticipated (made your guess by watching your partner for clues). Here are two tips to help you make your move.

Right/Left Drill *As in the high/low drill, call out "right" or "left," and move in that direction as soon as you can.*

1) Keep your feet moving. Imagine that the court is burning hot and you can't keep either foot on it for too long.

2) Your first step is always made with the foot that is closest to the ball. (If the ball is coming to your right, move your right foot first.) You may need to make an explosive, lunging step or some small, quick adjustment steps.

"Yes" Drill *If you have reacted quickly in the high/low drill and the right/left drill, you will be in the best spot to hit in your strike zone. This makes it much easier to hit the ball in the middle of your racket strings. Call out "yes" each time you achieve this.*

If you anticipate well, you'll find that your feet and body will be positioned well before the ball bounces, and you'll have plenty of time to hit the ball while it is still in front of you.

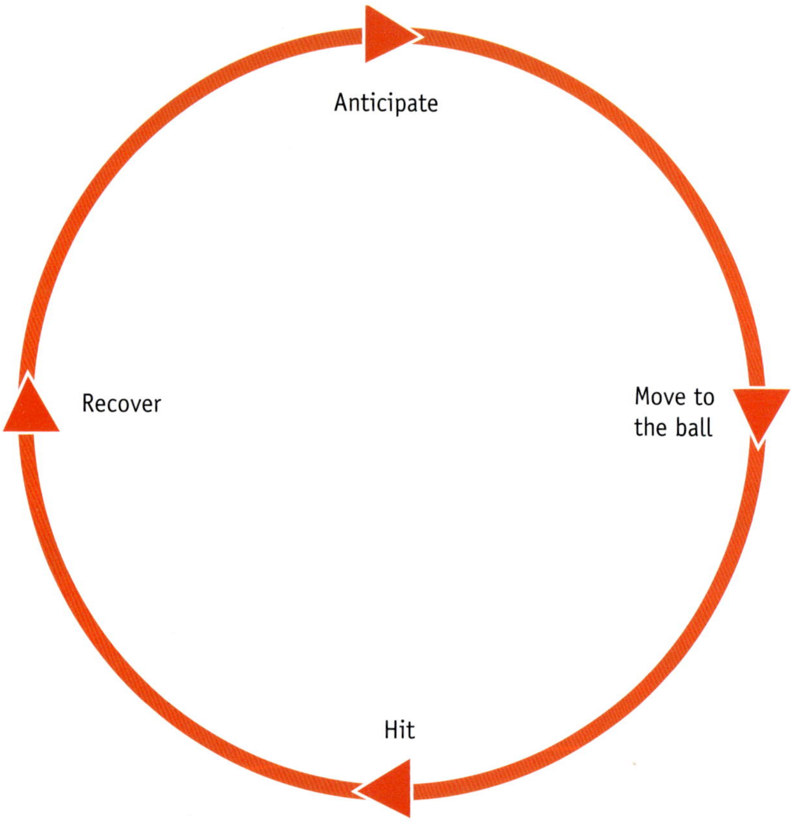

Anticipate, move to the ball, hit, recover. Tennis requires a continuous cycle of movement.

Hitting the Ball

So far you've been sending the ball in an arc over the net. That's great for rallying. When you start wanting to win points with your stroke, you'll find there are about a million different ways to send the ball. It's time to experiment again. You can use different grips, different racket swings and different stances. As a great player you will want to use many different shots...topspin, underspin, sidespin, flat, high, low, fast and slow. The information that comes next is a foundation for the different shots that you will use.

Let's take a more in-depth look at the four basic strokes every tennis player needs: the forehand, backhand, serve and volley. The forehand and backhand are called groundstrokes, because you hit the ball after it bounces on the ground. The serve is the stroke that starts every game of tennis, and a volley is when you hit the ball out of the air before it bounces.

Let's look at groundstrokes first. You'll hit a lot of these!

The Forehand

The forehand is a fancy name for hitting the ball with your palm forward. This should be familiar to you from all the palm-up drills. Usually the forehand is hit with your dominant hand gripping the racket.

How you hold the racket will ultimately determine the way in which you hit the ball. Professional players are constantly changing their grips to hit different shots.

Forehand Grips

There are three basic forehand grips.

1) The Eastern Grip—is sometimes called the "shake hands" grip. Imagine that you are shaking hands with

Eastern forehand grip

your racket. That is the position your hand will be in for an Eastern grip. It is a very popular grip because it is comfortable and versatile and makes it easier for you to hit many types of shots. The face of the racket will be looking toward the net and you will be hitting the ball slightly in front of your body.

2) Semi-Western Grip—With the Semi-western grip your hand is slightly underneath the racket. This is the most popular forehand grip on the professional tour. It is very effective for power forehands and topspin forehands.

3) The third main grip is the Continental. In the modern game this grip is used mostly for serves and volleys. However, you can sometimes find a player who uses the Continental grip for handling low balls and putting sidespin or underspin on the ball. From the "shake hands" grip, move your hand so the "V" made by your thumb and index finger is slightly to the left of center on the top edge of the handle (left-handed players, move the "V" slightly to the right).

Semi-western grip

Continental grip

If you are left-handed, hold up a mirror to the photos to see what the grip will look like in your hand.

Hold the racket firmly, but with a relaxed grip. Think of holding a baby bird. You don't want to squeeze it too hard or you'll hurt it, but you don't want it to fly away either.

Be a scientist and experiment with different grips. See what they do to the ball and how they feel in your hand. See if you can make the ball spin in different directions.

Forehand: 1) unit turn

2) impact

3) follow-through

Hitting the Forehand

When you've positioned yourself to hit the ball with your forehand, your shoulders should be turned and you should use your free hand to help guide your racket up and back. There are several different positions that your feet could be in: the open stance, the square stance and the semi-open stance.

The open stance is primarily used for the return of serve and for reaching wide balls. Your feet are more than shoulder width apart, and your front foot is a little bit closer to the net than your back foot.

You are in the square stance when your feet are more sideways to the net, with your back foot behind your front foot. The square stance is useful for shuffling forward to reach short balls, and backward for high, deep balls.

Any stance between the open and square stance is called the semi-open stance, and is just a variation that players use to position themselves well to hit the ball comfortably.

Now that your feet are in the right position, you're ready to start your forward swing. The butt end of the racket should be pointing toward the ball, with your wrist bent back and stable. Your eyes and head should still be facing forward, watching the approaching ball.

Just before the ball arrives, push up from the ground and turn your hips and shoulders forward. This will make your racket head move forward toward the ball. Making contact with the ball in front of your body, continue to rotate your hips and shoulders and extend your racket toward your target. The longer your racket travels toward your target (the "hitting zone"), the more you can control the direction of the ball.

After the ball has left your racket, stay relaxed and let your racket travel forward so that your elbow finishes high. This is called the follow-through.

Now you need to recover quickly and get ready for the next shot.

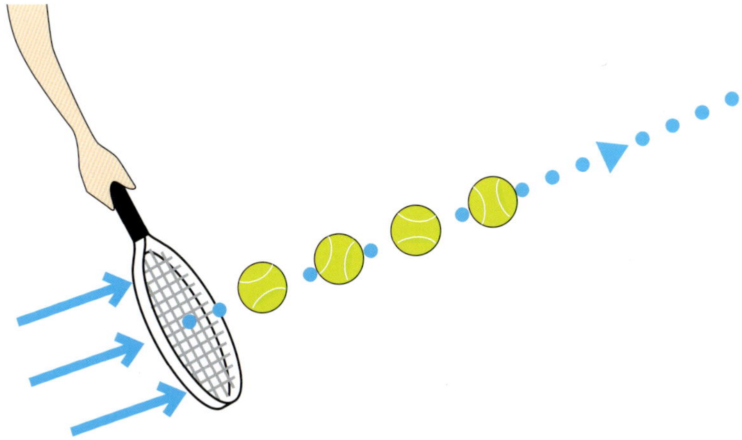

Staying in the hitting zone means keeping your racket moving forward on the same flight path as the ball for as long as you can. Imagine that you are hitting not just one ball, but four balls lined up.

Square stance

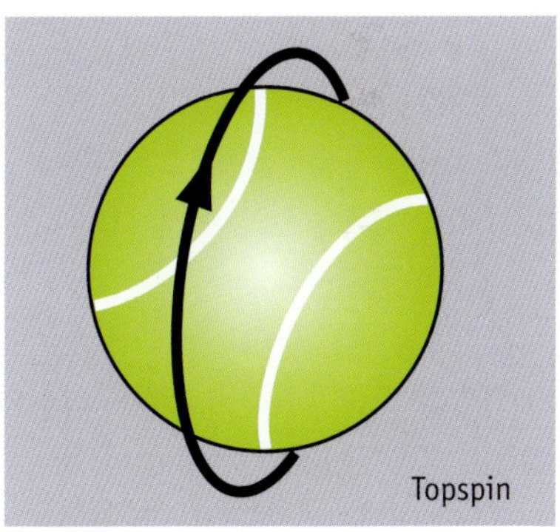

Topspin

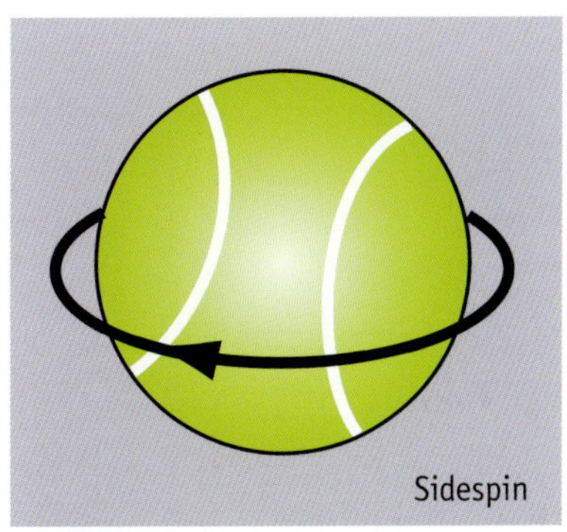

Sidespin

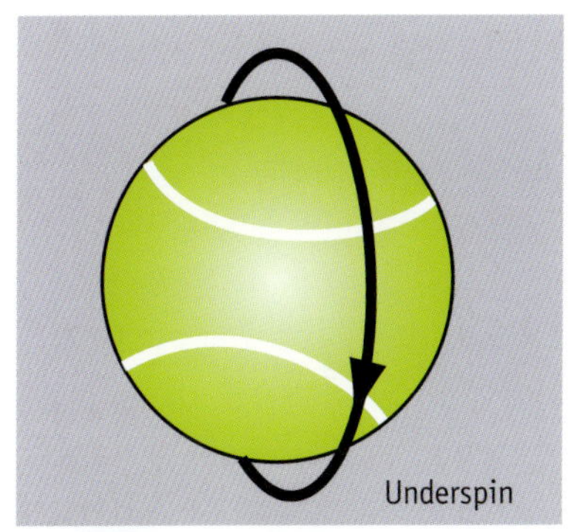

Underspin

Topspin: *The ball spins forward in the air as it travels away from you. To put topspin on a ball, you must drop your racket head well below the ball and swing upwards, brushing up the back of the ball, keeping the racket head moving in an upward path even after the ball has left your racket. The faster you swing up the back of the ball, the more topspin you will create.*

Sidespin: *The ball will rotate sideways in the air, right to left or left to right, like a Frisbee. To hit sidespin you start with your racket slightly above the ball and bring the strings down, across the back of the ball from right to left or left to right.*

Underspin: *The ball spins backward. Cutting from high to low behind the ball with your racket creates underspin.*

The Backhand

A backhand is a groundstroke that is hit on your non-dominant side. It is like the "palm down" shots you learned against the wall.

It is usually a good idea for younger players to learn the backhand using a two-handed grip. This will help give you extra strength to keep your racket stable. Some players start by using a two-handed backhand and later move on to a one-handed stroke as they get stronger, but there are still many professional players who prefer the two-handed stroke.

Backhand Grips

There are many backhand grips. We'll look at three: the two-handed, the Eastern and the Continental.

Eastern backhand grip

1) The two-handed backhand grip has many variations. Try using a Continental forehand grip and add your non-dominant hand on the grip, above your dominant hand. Your hands should be just touching each other but not overlapping. A slight variation of this can be used by moving your dominant hand into an Eastern or Semi-western grip.

2) With the Eastern backhand grip, the "V" of your hand is on the left edge of the handle and the knuckle of your index finger is on top. Spread your fingers out slightly for extra support and flexibility. (If you are left-handed, the "V" of your hand will be on the right edge of the handle.)

3) The Continental grip is the same as the one used for the forehand and, like the forehand, is used for hitting sidespins and underspins.

Two-handed backhand grip

Hitting the Backhand

We'll work on a two-handed backhand first. Once again you'll start in your ready position. When you see that the ball is coming to your backhand (your non-dominant side), use the unit turn to turn your shoulders and hips, drawing your racket back with both hands. Move your body into a position where you can comfortably hit the ball, preferably at waist height (remember your "strike zone"). The most popular stance is the square stance,

Backhand: 1) unit turn

2) impact

3) follow-through

with your front leg closer to the net and lined up with your back leg, but you can also use the open or semi-open stance on the two-handed backhand.

Your knees should be flexed so that you can push up as you turn your hips and shoulders forward, bringing your racket toward the impact point. Make contact with the ball in front of your body and extend your arms forward toward your target to have as long a hitting zone as possible. Keep your hips and shoulders rotating until your back shoulder ends up in front of your front shoulder.

Relax your arms for the follow-through, letting your racket travel forward and up.

Don't forget to recover. Get ready for the next shot right away!

Now try a one-handed backhand. Start with your non-dominant hand on the throat of the racket. It will help you to change your grip

One-hand backhand impact and follow-through.

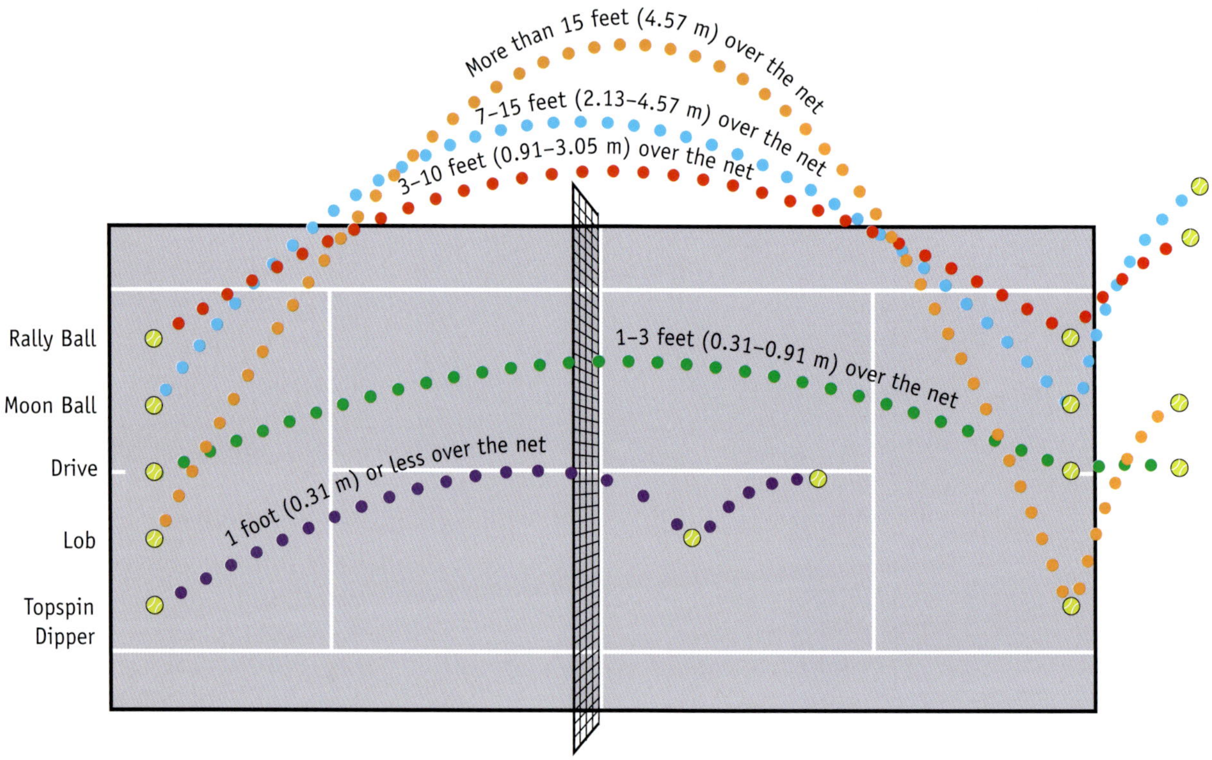

The ball can travel in many different arcs.

and draw the racket back. As the ball arrives, push up with your legs, release the racket from your non-dominant hand, and bring the face of the racket toward the ball, making contact in front of your body. Unlike the two-handed backhand, when hitting one-handed your hips and shoulders stop rotating when you hit the ball. Continue to keep the racket moving toward your target for as long as possible (the long hitting zone again). Relax to let the racket finish up high for your follow-through.

Shot Drills Now that you are rallying forehands and backhands, here are some shots you can work on:

Rally balls: This ball travels safely above the net and lands deep in the court. As long as your opponent is not at the net this is a very safe shot that will prevent your opponent from attacking you if it is hit well.

Moon balls: A moon ball travels very high above the net and lands deep. It bounces over your opponent's head, making it a safe shot that will often produce a weak return. This can be a useful shot when your opponent is on the baseline.

Drive: This ball is hit fairly flat, and travels quite low over the net. To hit this shot you must receive the ball above the level of the net so that you can level your swing and hit straight through the ball. This shot is used to force your opponent and to end points. It is a bit of a high-risk shot because it doesn't have very much clearance over the net.

Topspin dipper: This shot goes low over the net and sinks fast. It is really useful when your opponent is at the net and you want to force him or her to volley the ball up so that you can then put it away. This shot is also useful to hit on a sharp angle to make your opponent run.

Lob: This shot travels high over the net and lands deep in your opponent's court. It is a very safe shot and can get you out of trouble when your opponent is attacking the net.

Forehand and Backhand Drills

Receiving drill: See how many balls in a row you can receive in your strike zone. You get one point for each one. The first person to reach ten points wins.

Centering drill: See how many balls you can hit in a row on the sweet spot (the center) of your racket. Say "yes" every time you feel that you have hit the ball in the sweet spot.

Rally for consistency: See how many balls you and your partner can hit in a row. Remember, this is a cooperative drill, so you need to work together to succeed.

Rally in the alley drill

Rally in the alley: This is a great drill for working on direction. Stand in the alley, with your partner standing opposite you. Try to hit every ball so that it lands in the alley. Start near the service line and work your way back. Do the drill again in the other alley.

Match the arc: Working with a partner, send balls back and forth across the net, trying to match the arc of the ball you are receiving. For a variation on this drill, you can tie helium balloons to the net and pick one to hit your ball over.

Rallying with targets

"Rule #7, The Service: The server shall stand with both feet at rest behind the baseline and within the imaginary continuations of the centermark and sideline. The server shall then project the ball by hand into the air in any direction and before it hits the ground, strike it with his racket, and the delivery shall be deemed to have been completed at the moment of the impact of the racket and the ball."

Rally with targets: Set up targets crosscourt and down the line. This drill is great for singles and doubles. If you are training for singles, you should try to hit the ball a little higher over the net so that it goes deep into the court. If you are training for doubles you should keep your balls low over the net.

Lindsay Davenport has a great serve!

The Serve

Once you are ready to play a traditional game of tennis, the rules say that every point must start with a serve. Take a look at Rule #7, The Service, in the top right corner of this page.

The most important thing to know about the serve is that you've got to get it in the box! You can't win a point if you don't get your serve in.

Most players serve with an overhead action, but underhand serves are legal. You just have to remember that you must hit the ball out of the air. You cannot bounce it on the ground first or hit it straight out of your hand.

See what happens when you impact the ball in different places—over your head, in front of you, more to one side or the other. Where does the ball land? This is also a great way to experiment with serving the ball into different places in the box so that it is harder for your opponent to get it back.

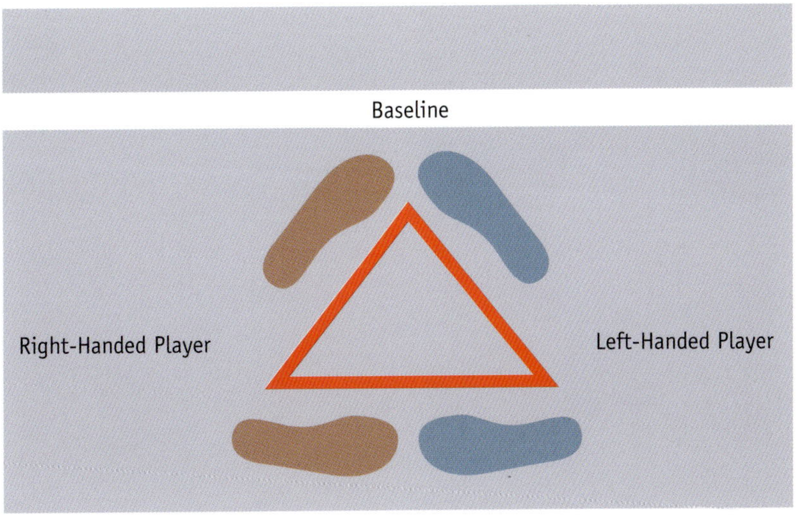

Foot positioning for a serve

Getting Set to Serve

You probably want to get playing, so let's work on a basic serve that will get you started.

Stand behind the baseline, to the right of the center mark. With your racket shoulder slightly behind your other shoulder, gently toss the ball over your head and extend your racket up so that you hit the ball in an upward arc, over the net and into the opposite service box. Develop a consistent rhythm by saying out loud "toss and hit" as you do so.

Beginning serve: 1) toss

2) reach

3) hit

Advanced serve: Step 1) starting position

Steps 2 & 3) check mark & bow position

Step 4) impact & extension

Step 5) follow through

Think back to the wall. Remember that the impact point controls the height and direction of the ball. Experiment with the impact point until you can get the ball to arc two to three feet over the net and land in the service box.

Stand to the left of the center mark and practice serving from there, too. Practice the serve until you can get the ball into the box on just about every try. Now you'll be able to play the official game of tennis! To find out about Scoring and Rules, look ahead to Chapter 7.

As your game progresses, you'll probably want to take your serve to the next level. Here are the five steps to a more advanced serve:

Step 1: Start behind the baseline, with your feet and shoulders facing sideways. Your feet should be shoulder-width apart, with your non-dominant shoulder, hip and ankle pointing toward your target. Think of having an imaginary triangle on the court. Place your feet on either side of the bottom triangle.

Hold the ball gently with all five fingertips of your non-dominant hand, palm facing up. Hold your racket loosely with an Eastern or Continental grip. Put both arms out in front of you, with the ball touching the racket face, pointing your arms in the general direction of the net post that you are facing.

This starting position allows you to hit the ball harder by increasing your racket speed as you rotate up to the ball.

Tossing drill

Step 2: Your ball hand extends up over your head, and you release the ball when it is at eye level, extending your arm straight up. As your racket gets back behind you, your elbow should bend. Your arms should now be in the check mark position.

Step 3: As you release the ball, you also bend your knees and begin to shift your weight forward. Push your front hip over the baseline. This will put your body into a "bow" shape. This loads up your large muscles (legs, stomach, shoulders) and prepares you to release that energy upwards toward the ball.

Step 4: Push up with your knees and throw your racket up at the ball, making sure that you keep your eyes on the ball. The ball should be tossed high enough to give you time to uncoil your body so that you throw your racket up at the ball and hit it with a fully extended arm. This will increase the speed of your serve.

Step 5: Relax. Let your racket continue to travel forward and down. Turn your hips and shoulders forward and allow the racket to finish beside your opposite hip.

Service Drills

The best way to get good at this more advanced serve is to break it down into easier steps. Here are a few drills that will help you to learn or improve your serve.

Tossing drill: It might seem like the toss is not very important because the racket is what gets the ball over the net, but if you don't have a good, consistent toss, you'll never have a good, consistent serve. A great way to practice your toss is to put your racket down in front of you as we've shown in the photo above left.

Stand in your serving position and toss the ball up as if you were going to serve. Use your shoulder to extend your arm up, instead of using your elbow. Your arm should stay fairly straight for the toss. When you release the ball from your fingertips it should have little or no spin. See if you can read the writing on the ball as it rises. Remember that it should go a bit higher than you can reach with your racket. When the ball comes down, it should land on your racket strings.

Two-ball drill

Two-ball drill: Another challenging exercise is to hold two balls, one in each hand. Stand in the service position. Toss

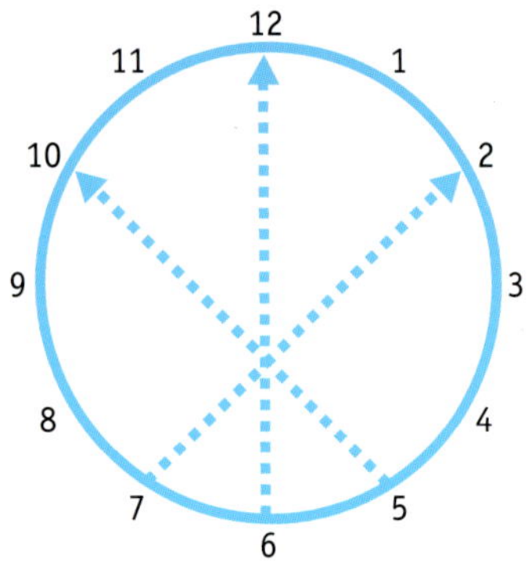

Think of a clock face when adding spin.

the ball up from your non-dominant hand (your tossing hand). Throw the other ball (from your racket hand) and try to hit the tossed ball. If you do this well, the thrown ball will hit the tossed ball, and the tossed ball will go over the net, just like it would if you served it. (If you miss the tossed ball, the thrown ball will go over the net, and that is okay, too...it helps you get the feel of throwing your racket up at the ball.)

Impact drill: The impact point (where the racket makes contact with the ball) is also very important. It controls the direction and height of the serve. If you don't impact the ball at the correct point, your serve will not work. To develop a good impact point, start in the check mark position that we described earlier. Toss the ball up and throw your racket up at the ball. Make contact in the middle of your strings, with your racket arm fully extended.

Adding Spin

Once you feel comfortable with the service motion, try adding spin to vary your serve. It is a great way to vary the height and the direction of the ball. There are many types of spin serves, but the two fundamental varieties are the slice and the topspin. If you get a chance to watch the pros, see if you can follow the path of their spin serves.

Try some spins yourself. To hit a slice serve you must carve up and across the back of the ball. Imagine that the ball has a clock face on it. If you are right-handed, you would be hitting the ball at 7 o'clock and brushing up to 2 o'clock. Left handed players hit at 5 o'clock and brush up to 10 o'clock. Players like to slice because it causes the ball to curve sideways and drop, allowing them to send the ball wider into the service box and pulling the returner farther off the court.

A topspin serve is similar to the slice serve, except that you brush the ball straight up (from 6 o'clock to 12 o'clock). In order to do this the ball must be farther over your head. Players like this serve because topspin pulls the ball down. This allows them to hit higher over the net but still have the ball bounce in the service box. When you use a topspin serve you are much less likely to hit the ball into the net. (Also remember that the higher the ball goes over the net, the higher it bounces. This can make a topspin serve more difficult to return. It will bounce above your opponent's strike zone.)

Top players will toss the ball in front of them and then move their bodies underneath the ball. You may want to start by tossing the ball a little more over your head so your body is already underneath it. As you improve you can move your toss more in front of your body.

As you watch and play more tennis you'll see that there are many unique styles used for serving. We've given you five steps to the foundation of an advanced serve. Now you're free to develop your own style and make your serve a force to be reckoned with.

The Volley

Way back when you were practicing "palm up" and "palm down" and playing against the wall you were

Prepare in a wider, lower stance.

Line your racket up with the oncoming ball for a forehand volley.

learning to volley. (That's when you hit the ball before it bounces.) Now that you are on the tennis court, it's time to take a closer look.

You can hit a volley from anywhere on the court, and you probably will, but most volleys are hit when you are close to the net. The closer you are to the net, the more likely it is that you will hit the ball before it bounces. Certain players, like Patrick Rafter, Pete Sampras, Andy Roddick and Serena Williams, rush to the net often so they can hit a volley, because they know that if they hit a good volley they are likely to win the point. You'll also get lots of chances to volley when you play doubles because you're often close to the net when the point is started.

Line up your racket for a backhand volley.

Volleying is fast and fun, but you must remember that because you are close to the net, you have less time to prepare for the oncoming ball. Hitting a successful volley at the net will very often require nothing more than blocking the ball back into your opponent's court. How hard can that be?

Step 1: Prepare

Because the action at the net happens so quickly, you must prepare your body for an explosive movement in any direction. Start in a slightly wider and lower stance than you use at the baseline, and make sure you are on the balls of your feet. When you see the ball coming, get your body to the ball as quickly as possible.

Step 2: Line up

Using an Eastern forehand or Continental grip, line your racket up with the oncoming ball as quickly as you can so that the ball will hit the center of your strings. When you learned the unit turn with your groundstrokes, you turned your hips, shoulders and feet. When volleying, you turn your hips and shoulders just slightly—you don't have time for more. Hitting the ball in the center of your racket strings is the key to consistent volleying.

Step 3: Control

The direction of your volley is controlled by the angle of your racket face at impact. Once again, the eyes of your racket should be looking at your target. If your strings are facing straight ahead, the ball will go straight ahead. This is where you'll want to hit the ball when you are warming up. But when you are playing a game, you'll want to hit the ball away from your opponent. Experiment with the angle of your racket face to see where you can direct your volley. You should be able to hit some great angles and really make your opponent run.

Sometimes you will have to volley the ball farther, especially if you are farther away from the net. At first, the easiest way to do this is by increasing the height of the ball. In order to increase the height of the ball, tilt the racket face up more. (Remember that the ball will go where the eyes of the racket are looking.) As you become more skilful you will also want to increase the speed. You must use your body to help create power. Use the modified unit turn and push off your back leg, making sure to land on your front heel. This will drive your body forward, allowing you to hit through the ball with more power.

You'll find that you will use the volley a lot when you play doubles. The traditional starting position in doubles has one player at the baseline line, either serving or receiving, and the other player at the net. As you know, the closer you are to the net, the more likely you are to be able to hit a volley. Experienced players look forward to hitting volleys because they know that it is an easy way to put the ball away.

At the advanced level of doubles, the server will come in to the net as soon as the serve has been hit. (This style of play is called "serve and volley.") Often the returning team will also be racing in to the net as soon as a good return has been hit. This leads to fast and furious volleying with all four players at the net. It is exciting to watch and even more exciting to play!

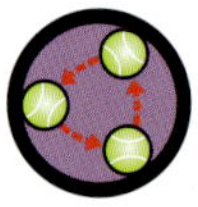

Volley Drills Start very close to the net with your partner close to the net on the other side. Hit the ball as low as possible over the net. If you hit the net, or the ball bounces before you hit it, you lose the point. Keep score and play up to ten.

Reflex volley drill: Both players stand across the net from each other, in the center of the service boxes. Volley back and forth, forehand to forehand for a while, and then backhand to backhand. Try

Practice volleying at targets near the baseline.

alternating forehand and backhand. See how many hits you can get in a row.

The volley game: Both players start just behind their own service lines. One player puts the ball into play by feeding it to the other player in the air. Both players then try to move closer to the net to put the ball away. You will quickly figure out that you must keep the ball low. If you send a high ball to your opponent, he will be able to put it away easily. If you hit low, it is more likely that your opponent, will have to hit up to get the ball over the net, and then you will be able to move in and put it away. Use half the singles court when doing this drill one-on-one. It is fun to use this drill for doubles, too, using the doubles court with four people.

Baseline volley: Very often you will be volleying a ball that is coming from your opponent's baseline. To develop your volley for this common situation, practice like this: Have your practice partner stand behind the baseline. You stand near the net, in the middle of the service box. Your partner should hit balls to you, and you must volley them back so that they land as close to the baseline as possible. It's fun to set up targets near the baseline, like cones or towels, that you try to hit. This will definitely help you with accuracy.

A variation on this drill is to volley from the service line. This will help you develop your serve and volley game.

With both variations, you can keep score by getting points for hitting a winning volley that your partner can't return. Your partner gets a point for hitting the ball past you. These drills are not only great for your net play, they are fun.

4/Specialty Shots

The groundstrokes, serve and volley are shots you will use over and over again. They are very important to the foundation of your game. But occasionally you'll find yourself in a position where a different kind of shot would be much more effective. Maybe your opponent will be at the net and you'll want to lob the ball high over his or her head, or your opponent will be way behind the baseline and you'll want to hit a dropshot just over the net. Or maybe you will be near the service line, with a high ball coming right to you. That's the perfect time to hit an overhead smash. These shots are called "specialty shots" and are ideal for these special situations. Remember there are many ways to hit a tennis ball, and you'll need to use them all to win points and games.

Serena Williams

Lob at impact

The Lob

There are several situations that you will be in where you will want to lift the ball in a high arcing shot over your opponent's head and deep into the back of the court. If you are in trouble, with your opponent attacking you at the net, if you are reaching wide for a ball, falling backwards off balance, hitting the ball out of your strike zone or just totally out of breath, you may choose to hit a lob.

This ball should travel high over the net and land near your opponent's baseline. To make this happen you have to prepare your racket very early. Get your racket behind or below the ball. Open the racket face so that the eyes are pointing up high over the net. Make contact with the ball in front of your body, lifting the ball up and following through smoothly in an upward path, finishing with your racket up high over your head. The high, smooth follow-through will help to ensure that your lob goes high.

Lob Drill Start at the baseline, with your practice partner standing across the net on the service line. Your partner sends you a ball that you must lob back over her head. She should reach up with the racket and make sure that the ball goes higher than the racket will reach. If you get it over your partner you win one point. If it lands within 3 feet (90 cm) of the baseline you get two more points. Play up to fifteen and then switch places. Remember to practice this with your forehand and your backhand.

The Overhead Smash

If your opponent hasn't perfected her lobs, you'll get lots of opportunities to hit overhead smashes. This is the ultimate offensive shot. It's a

Lob drill

definite crowd-pleaser and, if done properly, is one of the most satisfying shots to hit.

The first step to a good overhead is good positioning. Shuffling and turning to run back under the ball are the two most popular ways to get there. If you only have a few steps to take, shuffling works well. If there is more distance to cover, turning and running to get under the ball is usually faster.

The next step is your body preparation. Get into the same check mark position that you use with your serve. This should be done as soon as you see a lob go up. Use your non-dominant hand to help line yourself up with the ball. If you were to freeze in that position, the ball would hit your non-dominant hand.

Checklist:

1. Are you in a sideways position?
2. Are your arms in the check mark position?
3. Is the ball above you?
4. Will your arm be fully extended when you hit the ball?

Running back for an overhead

Shuffling back to get underneath the ball for an overhead

Reach up to impact

Snap and follow-through

If you answer "yes" to all four questions, then you are ready to go for it. Keeping your non-dominant hand up and your eyes on the ball, throw your racket up at the ball. Snap your wrist at impact, like you are cracking a whip. Follow through with a relaxed arm. The impact point controls depth and direction. If you have a good impact point, the ball will explode off your racket for a winner.

Overhead Progression Drill Here's a great drill that you can practice on your own, without a partner:

Step 1: Throw a ball up as high as you can with your non-dominant hand. Let it bounce, move under it and catch it again in your non-dominant hand, making sure that you are sideways in the check mark position. Do this five times, then try it without letting the ball bounce.

Step 2: Instead of catching the ball, reach up with your racket and just try to touch the ball in the center of your strings.

Step 3: Toss the ball up high, throw the racket head up to the ball and this time hit it over the net, using the wrist snap and follow-through.

Lob/Overhead Drill Have a partner lob the ball up to you and practice hitting an overhead. Then switch and lob to your partner. This is a great way for both of you to get practice on two of the most useful specialty shots you can hit. You can add excitement by playing out the point after an overhead has been hit.

Experiment with the impact point by noticing what happens when you hit the ball behind your head, directly overhead, a little in front of you or a lot in front of you. This will help you determine the ideal impact point for a smashing shot.

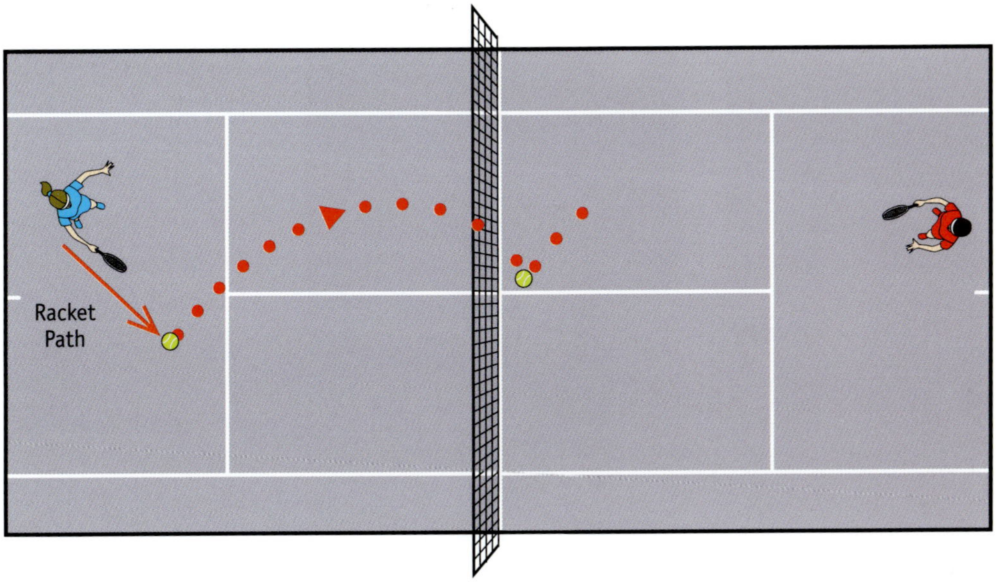

The path of a drop shot

The Drop Shot

The drop shot is a great shot to use if your opponent is hanging out deep in the backcourt. On a drop shot the ball finishes its arc just as it passes over the net, so that it drops on your opponent's side very close to the net. Underspin stops the ball from traveling forward, toward your opponent. Your opponent will have to run far and fast to get her racket on this ball!

Learning the drop shot involves patience. You really need to get a feel for the height and speed of the ball. And you'll often see some pretty surprising results.

Drop Shot Progression Drill

Step 1: Stand at the service line, sideways to the net. With your forehand grip, toss a ball gently from your non-dominant hand and brush your racket strings forward, underneath the ball, so that the ball spins backwards. When the ball bounces, it should come back to you. Try to hit it with enough underspin that it comes right back to you and you can catch it in your non-dominant hand again. That's a bit crazy, isn't it? Your racket moves forward and the ball bounces backwards.

Step 2: Once you've got the feeling of putting underspin on the ball and can catch it, try adding to the above exercise by shuffling forward after each hit and hitting the ball again with underspin, moving closer to the net each time. After about three hits you should be pretty close to the net. On your fourth hit try to make the ball go over the net and drop gently on the other side.

Step 3: Start at the service line again and make only two hits before you make the ball drop over the net from a little farther away. Then try it again, making the ball drop gently over the net from the service line. You'll notice that the ball has to have a slight arc to make it over the net.

Now try this shot using your backhand. Many people

Drop Shot Progression on Forehand Side

Step 1

Step 2

Step 3

Over the net!

find it easier to hit a backhand drop shot than a forehand. Use the same progression.

If you get really good at this, you'll be able to get the ball to bounce at least three times before it reaches your opponent's service line! You can try this shot from farther and farther away as you get more skilled.

As with the lob, you can really take your opponent by surprise with a drop shot. Try to be a master of disguise: Prepare your racket early, as if you were going to hit a normal groundstroke, then sneak in a drop shot. You'll have your opponent on the run. If your opponent does manage to return the ball, you can then hit a deep lob forcing her to dash back to the baseline. This combination of shots will tire your opponent out and win you many points.

Drop Shot Progression on Backhand Side

Step 1

Step 2

Step 3

Move the ball gently over the net.

What happens when your drop shot has so much underspin that it bounces on your opponent's side, then comes right back over the net before your opponent can even touch it? You win the point! Your opponent must touch the ball before it bounces for the second time. (This is the only situation in which a player is allowed to reach over the net to touch the ball.)

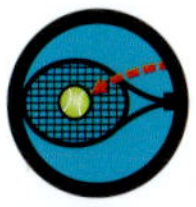

The perfect drop shot will arc on your side of the net, hit the cord on the top of the net and drop onto your opponent's court with little or no bounce. It is almost impossible to return!

Slide the ball into your foot...

and lift it up.

Pick-up Ball Drills If you've been practicing all the drills we've talked about, you've been hitting a lot of tennis balls.\ That means you've also been picking up a lot of tennis balls! You can always bend down and pick them up one by one with your hand, but if you really want to look like a pro, here are two tricks to learn:

1) Using the top edge of your racket head, slide the ball up against your shoe. Pull it up into the air by raising your foot and the racket, let it bounce and catch it. This is a good "advanced intermediate" move.

Tap the ball to make it balance.

Tap again and catch it.

2) To get even fancier, you can pick up a ball using just your racket. Holding your racket at a 45-degree angle, tap the ball with the top of your strings so that it bounces. Tap it one more time to make it bounce higher and catch it. Now you're really looking like a pro!

5/Strategy and Tactics

Now that you know how to hit the ball over the net in many different ways, it's time for you to think about how to win points with your shots. This is where strategy and tactics come into play. Strategy means having an overall plan or game style. Tactics are how you implement the strategy (how you make your plan work). A strategy in tennis can be as simple as hitting the ball over the net one more time than your opponent. The tactics behind this strategy might be to run every ball down, hit it high over the net and be determined to stay out on the court for as long as it takes. Bjorn Borg employed this strategy very successfully in the 1970s to win many professional titles.

Another strategy might be to win points as quickly as you can. Tactically, you could achieve this by hitting the ball as hard as possible and trying to end each point quickly.

Jennifer Capriati

Both strategy and tactics are needed when you start to play matches. When you are formulating an overall plan on how to win in any sport you should take into account three main factors: your personality, your technical skills and your physical ability.

There are three basic strategies in tennis.

1) The defensive baseliner
This player tends to be very patient and is fast on the court, able to get to many balls, has extremely dependable strokes and has the ability to defend well.

2) The aggressive baseliner
Always looking for a way to finish the point, this player is usually fast, with at least one powerful shot. When given a short ball or an easy ball, this player will try to end the point by hitting a winner.

3) The net rusher
A powerful serve or service return allows this player to rush into the net and immediately take up an attacking position. With a big serve, the net rusher forces opponents to hit weak returns. When the net rusher is returning a serve, his return forces the opponent to hit a weak shot that can be attacked at the net.

Here's a quick quiz you can take to give you an idea of the strategy you might be suited for:

1) I try to put the ball away quickly.

2) I am physically in great shape, with lots of endurance.

3) I like to see quick results.

4) I am willing to work for a long time to get results.

5) I can hit a good selection of powerful shots.

6) I love to try to return "impossible" shots.

7) My first serve is a weapon.

8) I use my serve to get a rally started.

9) If I get an easy ball, I try to end the point.

10) I love being at the net.

11) I love to hit hard from the baseline.

12) My return of serve often produces a weak shot from my opponent.

If you answered "yes" to 2, 4, 6 and 8, you are probably developing a defensive baseliner style of play.

If you answered "yes" to 1, 3, 5, 7, 9 and 11, you may be more suited to an aggressive baseliner style.

If you answered "yes" to 1, 3, 7, 10 and 12, you might want to focus on becoming a net rusher.

As you grow, and your game develops, you may switch styles of play several times. Many of the top players, although they have a certain style or strategy, are able to switch to a secondary strategy when necessary. Great players have the ability to attack, counterattack, defend and rally to help them implement their strategic plan.

Now that you have thought about a strategy that might suit you, it is time to think about how you will make your strategy work. We'll look at some tactics needed to employ each of the three basic strategies described above.

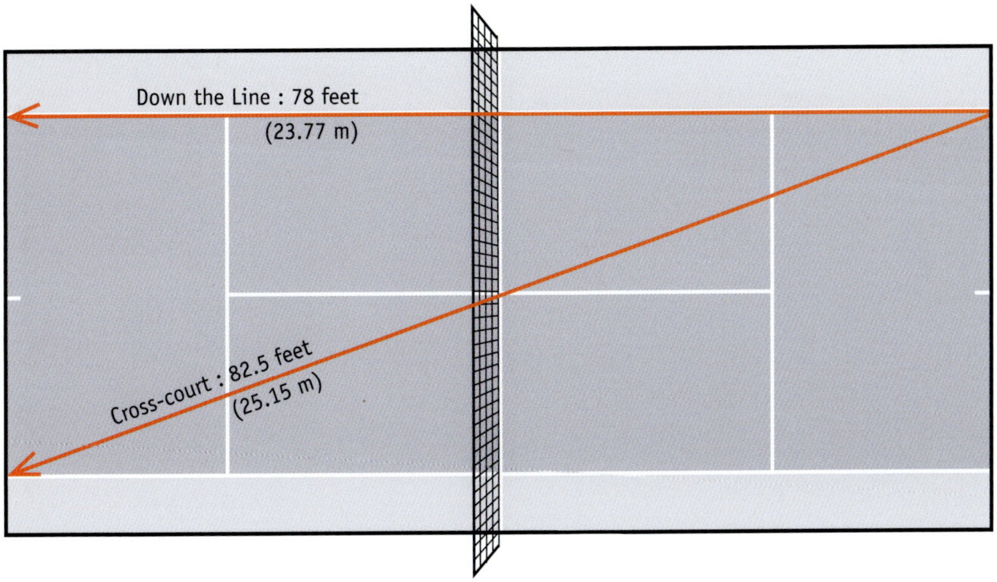

Play it safe: always try to hit cross-court.

Defensive Baseliner Tactics

Be consistent by hitting safe shots. The dimensions of the tennis court and the height of the net mean it is safer to hit the ball cross-court from the baseline. The net is lower at the middle and the court is longer diagonally from corner to corner, so you have more room for the ball to land in. Hitting the ball high over the net, deep into the opposite corner, will ensure that you do not make many errors, and will keep your opponent back behind the baseline, unable to attack you.

Be physically prepared to run every ball down and get every ball back. Remember that all you really need to do is hit the ball in one more time than your opponent to win the point. One of your biggest advantages with this tactic is that you will wear your opponent down physically and psychologically. Of course this means you must be physically and psychologically prepared to outlast your opponent in this situation.

Aggressive Baseliner Tactics

The aggressive baseliner likes to put the ball away as quickly as possible. Many of the top professional players use this strategy. The tactics they employ include hitting their power shots and exploiting their opponents' weaknesses. Here are some popular patterns of play:

The longest match ever played lasted 6 hours and 32 minutes. It occurred in 1982 between John McEnroe and Mats Wilander in a United States versus Sweden Davis Cup match. The longest women's match was just one minute shorter and included a second set tiebreaker that lasted 1 hour and 47 minutes, with one point of the tiebreaker lasting an incredible 29 minutes.

- Serve the ball wide, recover to an optimum position on the court in order to hit your strength shot and then hit that next shot into the open court

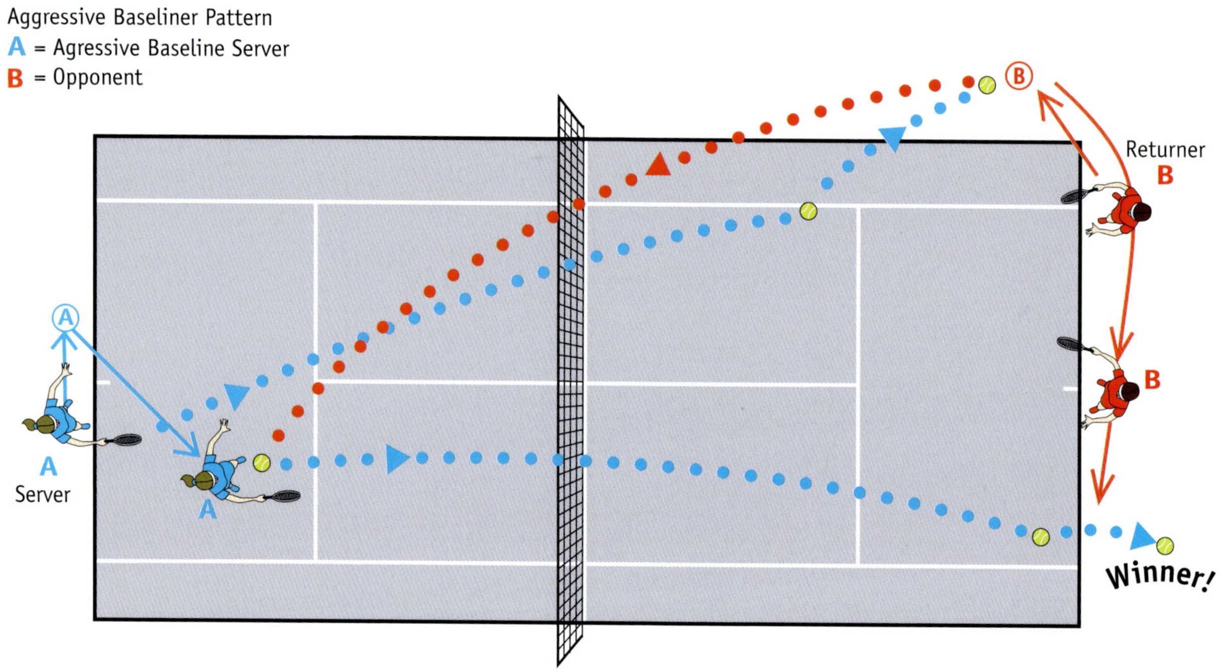

A serves out wide to B and recovers slightly to the left.
B returns cross-court and recovers to the left.
A hits a big forehand winner into the open court, out of B's reach.

(opposite to where you served the ball).

For example: You serve out wide to your opponent's forehand. He returns the serve down the middle and you move to your left so that you are in position to hit the ball with your forehand. You send the ball deep to your opponent's backhand corner, and he must run all the way across the court to hit the ball with his backhand, which is his weaker shot (see the diagram above).

- Serve the ball to the "T" (down the middle), recover to a position from which you'll be able to hit your strongest groundstroke, then drive the ball deep into your opponent's weaker side.
- Return the serve short and wide, then hit the next shot deep into the opposite side.
- Return a drop shot and move in, anticipating a short return, then either lob or pass your opponent with your next shot. This pattern is particularly effective with opponents who do not like to come to the net.

A "pattern of play" describes a specific shot, the recovery and the next shot after that.

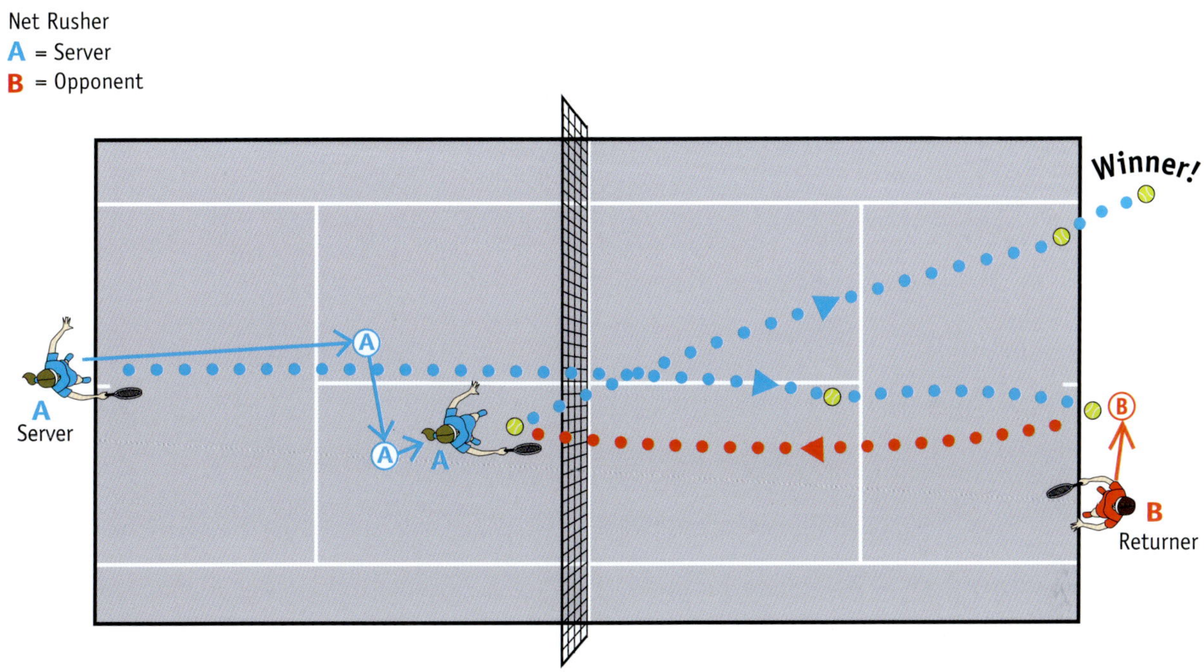

A serves to the "T" then moves in and volleys to the weaker side

The "T" is the area just to either side of the spot on the court where the service line and center service line intersect.

Net Rusher Tactics

This player wants to put his opponent under pressure right away. The tactics employed by this player involve serving or returning and then moving forward to take up an offensive position at the net.

Here are some examples of patterns of play:

- Serve out wide, volley into the open court.
- Serve to the "T," volley to your opponent's weaker side (see diagram).
- "Chip and charge": Hitting underspin on your return of serve so that the ball stays low, follow your return to the net and volley into the open court.
- "Drive and charge": Hitting a hard, deep return, follow it to the net and volley into the opposite corner.

Service Drill *Next time you are working on your serve, instead of just trying to get it into the box, work on serving it out wide so that you can run the pattern of serving out wide and hitting into the open court.*

The last two tactics we covered involve two shots. If the ball comes back to you for a third shot, what should you do? *Keep it simple!*

If you are running, reaching or off balance, hit the ball back into the center of your opponent's court.

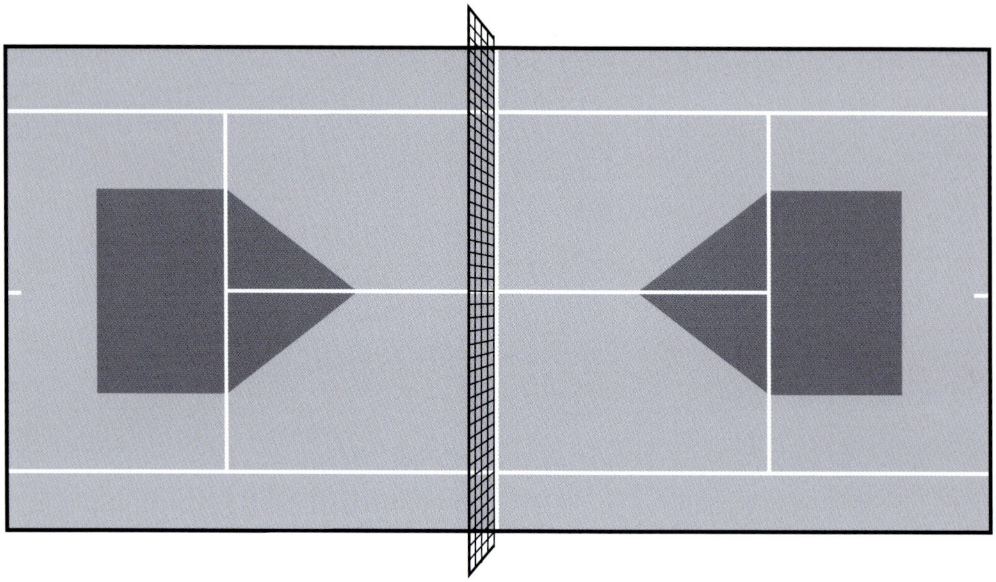

Imagine there are two houses on the court.

If the ball is in the center of *your* court, hit a shot that will put your opponent under pressure.

One of my favorite ways to work on this tactic is to imagine there is a house on either side of the net, in the middle of the tennis court. The house then becomes a target, either to hit into, or avoid. When you are working on consistency, aim for the middle of the house. If you are in trouble and stretching to reach the ball, aim for the middle of the house. However, if your opponent's ball lands in your house, try to hit it back out of your opponent's house. You'll notice that you will be able to win the point more often when you hit "out of the house." It will be difficult for your opponent to return the ball because you'll be making him run, or your ball will be deep, pushing him back.

If you find yourself in a baseline battle remember, when being defensive hit "into the house." And when you have the chance, with the ball comfortably in your house *and* in your strike zone, hit it "out of the house"!

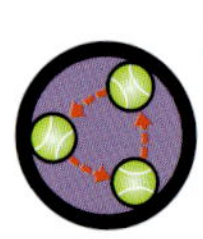

Rally Drill *Your partner must hit all his shots into your house. You must hit all your shots out of your partner's house. See who wins fifteen points first. Who works harder? Now switch and see what the results are.*

Your strokes are the tools that will allow you to implement your tactics, which will then enable you to have a winning strategy. The better your strokes become, the better your tactics can be. The best way to work on your strokes at this stage is within a tactical plan. Keep your plan in mind as you work. Think tactically before you think technically. In other words, you have to know what you want to do with the ball before you can practice doing it.

When I was young and learning to play, I used to pretend I was John McEnroe, and I would charge the net whenever I could, with reckless

A lob is a great weapon for a defensive baseliner.

It's no fun to have to practice with just a few balls—you'll be spending more time chasing after balls than hitting them. Try to gather a bucket of balls for practicing. They don't have to be new, but when they really don't bounce well anymore, make a dog happy by tossing them his way.

abandon. Other days I would be Bjorn Borg, and I would hit all my shots with lots of topspin and try to keep the rally going until my best friend, and opponent, would finally miss. Who is your favorite player? Andy Roddick, André Agassi, Serena Williams, Justine Henin-Hardenne? Watch the pros in action and determine their strategies. Then take your imagination and racket to the court. Have fun...keep searching for your game style. Ultimately, your tennis personality will come through in your choice of strategies. Who knows, maybe one day young players will be imagining they are *you*!

6/Doubles

We have mostly been talking about tennis as it is played between two people, called singles. You can also play tennis with four players, with two players teamed up on either side of the net. This is called doubles. Having four people on the court can lead to four times the fun!

You can flip forward to Chapter 7 for rules and scoring in doubles.

The main thing to remember about doubles is that you and your partner have to work together as a team. One of the best ways to do this is through constant communication. If you and your partner are moving and grooving together, you'll cover the court better, and the wins will start coming your way.

Mary Pierce and Martina Hingis

The starting positions for doubles

Doubles Strategies

Here are some strategies to help get you started:

1) Attacking the net
This strategy is used by most of the top professionals, as well as most high-level club players. They find that the easiest place to win the point in doubles is at the net, so they will move into the net as a team as soon as they can.

2) Both players back
This strategy is considered very defensive and is rarely used at the professional level. But sometimes your opponent's aggressive play at the net forces you into this defensive position. You might find this strategy helps when you are unable to put the ball away at the net or your opponents force you to stay back with good lobs. If the players on the baseline have penetrating groundstrokes and excellent lobs, this strategy can be successful.

3) One up and one back
This strategy is rarely seen at the professional level. Have you ever heard the saying "united we stand, divided we fall"? Well, that's what can happen with one up and one back. Because we don't always have all the weapons that the professionals have, we are sometimes forced to use this strategy. You might want to try this if one of you is comfortable covering the net while the other covers lobs from the baseline, especially if your opponents aren't very aggressive at the net.

You may choose to change your strategy throughout a match. If you know that you have options, you can talk with your partner and change a strategy that isn't working.

Daniel Nestor and Mark Knowles are among the world's best doubles teams!

Tactics for Doubles

It is very important for a doubles team to work together to implement their strategy. There are many sequences of shots, or "patterns," that are useful with the above three strategies. We'll look at one pattern for each of the three strategies.

1) Attacking the net

The service team has the first opportunity to attack the net. The server's partner can start at the net. A good server will communicate to the net person where the serve will land. This enables the net person to move into an ideal position to intercept the return of serve.

At the same time, after the serve is struck, the server will move forward to intercept any ball that the net person is unable to reach. Both players should have specific shots in mind, depending on the ball they receive. For example, if the return comes to the net person from a wide serve, the net person will automatically volley the ball down the middle. If the return gets past the net person and goes to the server, the server will hit low balls back crosscourt and high balls down the line. Having a plan eliminates decision making, allowing the attacking team to stay calm in the heat of the point.

There are many other patterns of play that the serving and returning teams can employ to maximize their chances to get the ball at the net. Creative attacking teams are coming up with more sophisticated tactics all the time, such as poaching, faking, I-formation and poaching off the return of serve, just to name a few. (Check the Glossary for definitions.) A

In 2002, the world's #1 ranked doubles team was Daniel Nestor of Canada and Mark Knowles of the Bahamas.

The net team attacks, while the baseline team defends.

good attacking team communicates well together, and both players are hungry to get the ball at the net.

2) Both players back

Players who stay on the baseline often use driving/lobbing tactics. They will most commonly drive the ball down the middle, down the line, or right at the opponent's body, hoping to force them to miss. They may also lob over the net person's head.

Communication is critical when you are both playing back, so that you know who will cover balls down the middle.

3) One up and one back

This strategy includes a combination of tactics from the net attackers and the baseline players. The net player in this situation is hungry for the ball and tries to capitalize on every opportunity to get the ball at the net. The baseline player uses a combination of drives and lobs to protect the net player and try to set up an easy put-away for her partner.

What happens if a player is close to the net and her opponent hits a ball into the net so that the net is pushed into the player and it touches her? (The opponent's ball does not go over the net.) The opponent wins the point! You are never allowed to touch the net during a point, even if the net reaches out and touches you!

Communicating is one of the most important aspects of playing doubles.

Professional teams employ all three tactics successfully. Experiment with all of them and find out which is best for your team.

Whatever strategy you choose, it is absolutely imperative that you communicate with your partner about what serve you are going to hit, where your return will go and when you might try a lob. If you and your partner communicate and work together as a team, you will have a greater chance of success, and much more fun.

If you swing at a ball and your racket hits it twice (you "bobble" the ball), the hit is legal, but you may not intentionally hit a ball twice, nor are you allowed to catch it or carry it on your strings during a point.

7/Rules

The most important things to know about any sport are its rules. Remember, you can play tennis any way you want, as long as you and your opponent agree on the rules before you start. As you learned in Chapter 2, you can play a great non-competitive game of tennis against a wall, or a mini-tennis game using only part of the court. These sorts of games don't necessarily need rules.

When you feel you are ready to tackle the official game of tennis, however, the following pages will tell you all you need to know.

Monica Seles

Who was the winner of this tennis match?

Game, Set, Match!

Tennis scoring goes like this:

You need to win four points to win a game.

When you win six games, you have won the set.

To win the match, you need to win two out of three sets. (At the Grand Slam tournaments, the men need to win three out of five sets.)

SCORING

No score:	Love
First point:	15
Second point:	30
Third point:	40
Fourth point:	Game

The server's score is always called first. So if the server wins the first point, the score would be 15–love.

If the score is tied at 40–40 (each player has won three points), it is called deuce. A player must then win two points in a row to win the game. If the server wins the first point after deuce, the score is "Advantage Server" (or "ad in"). If the receiver wins the first point after deuce, the score is "Advantage Receiver" (or "ad out"). If the player who had the advantage wins the next point, he or she wins the game. If not, the score goes back to deuce.

The first player to win six games by a margin of two games wins the set. If the game score gets to five each, you play two more games. If one person wins both games, the set is over, with the score at 7–5.

If the game score gets to 6–6, you need to play a tiebreaker. The first player to win seven points, by a two-point margin, wins the

Who would start serving in the next set after a tiebreaker has been played? Since the tiebreaker is counted as a game, whoever started serving the tiebreaker is said to have served a game. Therefore, in singles, the player who served first in the tiebreaker would receive in the first game of the next set. In doubles, the team who started serving in the tiebreaker would be the receiving team in the first game of the next set.

André Agassi adds another trophy to his collection.

tiebreaker. The tiebreaker is scored with numerical scoring (1, 2, 3, etc.). The serving order stays the same, with the first point of the tiebreaker served from the deuce court. The other player then serves two points, the first from the ad court, the next from the deuce court. The first server then serves the next two points, again starting in the ad court. This continues until one player wins at least seven points by a margin of two points, for example 7–0, 7–5, or even 15–13. The players switch ends after every six points. Winning the tiebreaker is counted as a game. For example, the set score would be reported as 7–6, with the actual score of the tiebreaker in brackets.

This sounds a bit confusing at first, but after you've played a few tiebreakers it starts to make sense.

Can a tiebreaker go on indefinitely? Yes! There is no limit to the number of points that can be played in a tiebreaker. In a 1985 doubles match the tiebreaker lasted 50 points, with a final score of 26–24!

No Advantage

To keep the matches moving along more quickly, players will sometimes be asked to play "no ad" scoring. This means that if a game gets to deuce, there will only be one more point played in that game. The receiver gets to choose which side to receive the serve on, and the winner of that point wins the game. "No ad" scoring definitely speeds up most matches because in regular scoring games can technically go on forever if neither player wins two points in a row after deuce.

Now lets get down to the details. Here's how the rules are put into play:

Spin the racket to choose server and receiver.

Choice of Server and Receiver

This can be done with the toss of a coin or the spin of a racket. Check the butt of your racket. There is usually a letter or symbol on it. You can spin the racket on the ground or in your hand, covering the butt. Your opponent calls "up" or "down" while the racket is spinning. Then you check the butt to see which way the symbol has landed—right way up, or upside down. The winner can choose from one of the following:

1) which end to start on;
2) to serve first;
3) to receive first; or
4) to let the opponent make the choice.

Serving

The server must start from behind the baseline, on the deuce court side, between the center mark and the right-hand sideline. The serve must land in the opposite service box on the first bounce. The server has two chances to get the serve in. If the first serve doesn't go in, it is called a fault and the server may serve again, from the same side. If the second attempt isn't good, it is called a double fault, and the point is awarded to the receiver. The server then moves to the ad court side and serves again for the next point.

Remember to keep your feet behind the baseline when serving. Otherwise, you may be guilty of a "foot fault" and your serve would not be legal. If the serve touches the net on its way over and still lands in the service box, it is called a "let" and the serve is replayed.

Foot fault on the serve

No foot fault here!

The server is allowed to serve underhand, as long as the ball is tossed from the non-racket hand. Other rules, such as foot faults, still apply.

At the end of the first game the server becomes the receiver, and the receiver becomes the server.

After a serve, the ball must be allowed to bounce in the correct service box before the receiver hits it. In other words, you cannot volley a serve. During a rally, the ball can be hit out of the air (after it has crossed over the net) or after one bounce.

You win a point by hitting a ball into your opponent's court that your opponent cannot return into your court before the second bounce.

What happens if, when serving, the server lets go of his racket and it touches the net either before the ball has touched the ground or after it has bounced inside the service box? The server loses the point because the racket touched the net while the ball was in play.

What if the serve had already bounced outside the service box? This would just be a fault because the ball was out of play before the racket touched the net.

It is important to fuel up on breaks.

Receiving

The receiver may stand anywhere on his side of the court. The ball must bounce before the receiver hits it. The receiver must call a fault immediately if the serve is not good, or call a let if the serve hits the net then bounces in.

There is a rule that states that the receiver must play to the reasonable pace of the server. This means that if you are receiving you must get ready, but the server may not purposely speed up and serve before the receiver is ready.

Rules for Doubles

In doubles there are two players on each end of the court. The rules remain the same, except as follows.

The outer sidelines are used, so the court is wider. (The service box is still the same.)

Players take turns serving. The coin toss is the same. The team that will be serving (let's call them Team A) may choose which partner will serve first. In the next game the other team (Team B) may choose which of the two partners will serve first. In the third game, Team A will be serving again,

Taking Breaks: *During matches and tournaments, there are specific times allowed for breaks. At the end of each set you may take a break for a maximum of 120 seconds. Between points you have a maximum of twenty to twenty-five seconds (depending on the tournament) before the ball must be put into play again.*

Players are allowed to have a three-minute time out for a treatable medical condition. (You are not allowed to take a time out to recover your breath or strength.)

You usually have a five- to ten-minute warm-up period before the start of a match.

but the other partner must serve; and in the fourth game Team B's other partner will serve. This serving order then remains the same until the end of the set. At the beginning of the next set, the team whose turn it is to serve may again choose which partner will serve first. Once each person has served, the order will remain the same until the end of the set.

Partners must also decide which side they will receive the serve on, the deuce court or the ad court. Once a player has received on one side, he or she must continue to receive on that side until the next set.

After the service return, either partner may hit the ball at any time and may move anywhere on the court, as long as they don't cross over the net.

The tiebreaker in doubles works the same way as in singles. The servers keep going in order until the tiebreaker is finished.

After every odd game (after 1, 3, 5, 7 games, etc.) the players change ends. This is important when you are playing outdoors on a sunny or windy day. When changing ends you have a maximum of ninety seconds before you must start play again. (After the first game of each set, and during a tiebreaker, you do not rest on the end changes.)

We've covered the main rules and scoring procedures here. There are many other interesting rules for tennis that you might want to learn. You can find a complete list of the official International Tennis Federation rules by contacting any of the tennis associations listed at the back of this book.

Coaches' earnings: *Players in the top fifty rankings pay their coaches $1,000 to $1,500 per week. The coach of a top-ten player makes about $5,000 to $6,000 a week, plus expenses, and a bonus of 10 to 15 percent of the player's prize money. There's definitely incentive for coaches to get their players to move up in the rankings!*

8/Etiquette

There is more to playing a proper game of tennis than just following the rules. In tennis there are unwritten rules called etiquette, which explain to players how to be a "good sport." Etiquette was developed in response to a desire for fair play and politeness on the court. Etiquette is not hard to learn because it is mostly just common sense. For instance, etiquette dictates that you must wait until a point on the court beside you has finished before you go onto that court to retrieve a ball, or before you return one of their balls to them. (It would be rude and maybe dangerous to interrupt a point by going onto another court. And if you return a ball while people are still playing, they might step on it.)

Arantxa Sanchez Vicario and Martina Navratilova

Always be a good sport on the court!

In 1976 a "Code of Conduct" was developed by professional organizations to address some of the more common etiquette issues that arise during competitive tournaments. The Code of Conduct covers racket abuse, verbal abuse, ball abuse, gamesmanship, time violations, clothing violations, coaching during the match and much more. Failure to follow the Code of Conduct in a tournament can result in point penalties, game penalties or a match default. Most state or provincial tennis organizations will be able to supply you with a copy of the Code of Conduct. (Check at the back of the book for the organization in your area.)

Why do we need a set of rules about how we act on the court? Because players sometimes forget that tennis is a game, and a game is supposed to be fun. They think that they must win at all costs or that winning is the most important thing. This can lead to unsportsmanlike behavior... if they're not winning they cheat, swear, cry, throw things and generally behave pretty badly. Many of the rules in the Code are there to stop people from bad behavior or cheating.

If there is an interruption in the middle of the point, such as a ball rolling onto your court from another court, then the whole point should be replayed. This is also called a "let."

When you are playing tennis without the benefit of an umpire or referee, each player's obligations include:

- Following the agreed-upon rules of the game (mini-tennis, no ad scoring, first to eight games, or whatever else you agree on in conjunction with your opponent);

- Respecting players on other courts (keeping your noise level to a minimum, attempting to keep the balls on your own court);

- When serving, always calling out the score before each point is started;

- Calling all balls as fairly as possible, giving your opponent the benefit of the doubt (if you are unsure, or do not see the ball clearly land out, you must call it in);

- Shaking hands with your opponent after a match—win or lose!

- Leaving the court in a tidy condition, with all balls picked up before your court time ends.

If you do not agree with a line call made by your opponent, you may question it in a polite manner, for instance by saying, "Are you sure?" This will give your opponent an opportunity to change the call if she wasn't sure, but it is up to you to call all balls on your side of the net, and up to your opponent to call all balls on her side of the net. Of course, you should always try to call the ball fairly, and you must give your opponent the benefit of the doubt if you are not sure. Remember, if you did not clearly see that the ball was out, then you must call it in.

There are, of course, many more rules of etiquette. Just remember, etiquette always involves common sense and good manners. Keep in mind that tennis is a game, for fun. If you win, great! If you lose, no problem, you've probably learned a lot, you will get better and most importantly... you played! Have respect for yourself, your opponent and the game, and you will be a winner.

9/Tournaments

Once you get confident with your tennis skills and you know the rules and etiquette of tennis, you may want to test yourself against other players. You can do this by entering a tournament.

A tournament is organized so that players who are at a similar level can compete against each other. Most tournaments are "single elimination," meaning that once you lose a match, you're out of the tournament. There are more and more tournaments now for junior players that guarantee at least two matches. This gives you a chance to practice your skills and meet new opponents.

Lindsay Davenport and Martina Hingis

Event: ____________ Location: ____________ Date: ____________

Name	First Round	Second Round	Third Round	Fourth Round	Seeded Players

1. **1st Seed**
2.
3.
4.
5.
6.
7.
8. **7th or 8th Seed**
9. **5th or 6th Seed**
10.
11.
12.
13.
14.
15.
16. **3rd or 4th Seed**
17. **3rd or 4th Seed**
18.
19.
20.
21.
22.
23.
24. **5th or 6th Seed**
25. **7th or 8th Seed**
26.
27.
28.
29.
30.
31.
32. **2nd Seed**

Seeded Players

1.
2.
3.
4.
5.
6.
7.
8.

A sample draw sheet for a tournament, showing the placement of the seeds.

The Davis Cup

There are many different levels of competition available to a tennis player. Most local clubs will have at least one tournament a year, often called the Club Championship. Tennis organizations, such as provincial, state, national and international organizations, also run many tournaments. At the back of this book is a list of the organizations you can get in touch with to find out more about tournaments and other tennis information in your area.

There are also team tournaments played in many high schools and colleges. These usually include singles and doubles.

There are two international team tournaments that are very famous. The Davis Cup, named after Dwight Davis, is played by teams of men from various countries. The women's team event is called the Federation Cup (or the Fed Cup, as it is more commonly known). Each match won counts for a point, with the winning country gaining the most points overall.

Draw: Entrants names are put into a hat (or a box, or a computer) and are randomly *drawn* to see who will play against whom. In regular tournaments, the draw size varies, with anywhere from eight to 128 people allowed to enter.

Seeds: In many tournaments a number of the best players will be "seeded" so that they will not meet up with each other until the later rounds. The seeded players are spread out in the draw. The number of players to be seeded depends on the size of the draw.

Bye: If the number of entries in a tournament is uneven, one or more players will receive a "bye" in the first round. The byes would be given first to the seeds, in order, and then to any other player through a random selection.

Wildcard: Sometimes a player is allowed to enter a tournament even if he doesn't qualify in advance. This is often done if the player is just coming off an injury.

There are four major international tournaments that are affectionately known as "Grand Slam" tournaments. They are the Australian Open, the French Open, the British Open (usually called Wimbledon) and the U.S. Open. If a player wins each of these tournaments in one calendar year, he or she is said to have won the "Grand Slam."

10/Nutrition—Eat to Compete!

Professional tennis players today are stronger, fitter and faster than ever before. This is partly due to advances in physical training and nutrition. The old saying "you are what you eat" certainly holds true for tennis players.

Healthy eating fuels a healthy body, so when you step onto the court, you'll be ready to hit that ball... ONE MORE TIME! But what is healthy eating, and when should you eat what?

The good news is, you get to enjoy a variety of foods. Your body needs more than fifty different nutrients each day. You will benefit from nutrients such as protein, carbohydrates, fat and many different vitamins and minerals such as vitamins C and A, iron and calcium from a variety of foods.

Mary Pierce

Serving up a healthy diet

Protein comes in many forms. It has lots of jobs in our bodies, including building and repairing body tissues. Good sources of protein include lean meats such as beef, poultry (chicken), pork, fish, eggs, split peas, beans and lentils.

Carbohydrates, such as whole grains, fruits and vegetables, give your body energy, along with vitamins, minerals and fiber. Fresh fruits and vegetables are quick and easy snacks. Choose whole wheat when you are going to eat bagels, pita bread or spaghetti. Oatmeal and cereals can also be a good source of fiber.

We need fat in our diets to help supply energy for intense and long-lasting physical activities and to help digest fat-soluble vitamins. Fat in our diet usually comes from fats and oils such as salad dressing, butter, margarine, mayonnaise and sauces, as well as dairy products, nuts, meat and fish. Fat is naturally present in many other foods, so you usually don't need to seek out fat to add to your diet.

Vitamins and minerals are found in most foods. Different fruits and vegetables, along with other foods, have different vitamins and minerals. This is why variety is very important.

Okay, now you know *what* to eat, but *when* should you eat all this?

In general you should allow time for your meal to digest before a competition or a workout. Digestion times go like this:

Large meal	three to four hours
Small meal	two to three hours
Snack	one to two hours

A banana is a good, quick snack.

Breathe! Your muscles need oxygen to work properly, and so does your brain. When you get into a tight, competitive situation, the stress can cause you to breathe rapidly, but not deeply. Try to calm yourself down with slow, steady breaths.

You should avoid sugary foods forty-five to sixty minutes before a competition or workout. It is a myth that they will give you quick energy.

Ideal pre-competitive meals, eaten two to four hours before an event include:

- Cold cereal, skim milk and a banana
- Hot cereal with applesauce
- Homemade soup with crackers and skim milk
- Pasta with tomato sauce and skim milk
- Lean meat sandwich, no butter, banana and skim milk
- Whole wheat bread with peanut butter, fruit and skim milk

Drink on every changeover.

Tennis will make you sweat!

Be Sure to Drink Lots of Water

Water is the most important nutrient for athletes. Water makes up about 70 percent of muscle, or 60 percent of body weight, and is essential for transporting nutrients to cells and removing waste products from cells.

Dehydration occurs when the body loses too much water. It can lead to fatigue and increase the chance of cramps, heat exhaustion or heat stroke. You need to drink about 80 ounces (2.4 L) of fluids a day, and about 35 ounces (1 L) during each hour of play.

When you exercise, you lose fluids, especially on hot days, when you sweat more. Don't wait until you're thirsty to drink! Try to keep up your fluid intake before, during and after you exercise. Even slight dehydration can impair your physical performance and affect your brain, impairing your decision-making skills. If you are exercising for an hour or less, water is the ideal drink to keep you hydrated. If your session will last more than an hour, you might want a drink that has some sugar and electrolytes in it, as well, such as a sports drink.

You need your brain *and* your body to be in top shape for tennis.

Talking Tennis

Ace A winning serve that is not touched by your opponent.

Advantage The point after deuce is called "advantage." The players or umpire calling the score will often add the name of the player who won the deuce point, for example "Advantage Roddick." Players often shorten this to "ad," and call "ad in" if the server won the deuce point and "ad out" if the receiver won the deuce point.

Alley The area between the singles and doubles sidelines (in the U.K. it's also known as the tramlines).

Amateur A player who does not earn money playing tennis.

Backhand A shot that is hit on your non-dominant side, generally with the back of your racket hand facing the net.

Bagel Slang for zero, as in "I bageled him (6–0, 6–0)." A bagel is also a good pre-match snack that supplies carbohydrates.

Break Used to describe a situation where the receiver wins the game. Also called a service break.

Break point The point in the game where, if the receiver wins the next point, he or she will win the game.

Bye Used when the number of entries in a tournament is uneven, forcing the organizer to give a player a berth in the second round without the player having to play a first-round match.

Code of Conduct Developed in conjunction with professional tennis organizations to address some common rules of etiquette.

Cross-court A shot that travels diagonally across the court.

Davis Cup The men's international team competition, named after Dwight Davis.

Dehydration Occurs when your body does not have enough fluid to function properly.

Deuce A scoring term that indicates that the players are tied, with each player having won at least three points (score is 40–40).

Down the line A shot that travels over the net in a straight line, near one of the sidelines.

Draw The term used to describe all the entries in a particular tournament.

Drop A shot that lands just over the net.

Face The strung area of the racket.

Faking In doubles, when the server's partner pretends to be moving to attack the return of serve.

Fault A serve that does not land in the service box. A double fault is the second serve that does not land in the box.

Federation Cup Also known as the "Fed Cup," this is the women's international team competition.

Fifteen The first point in a game (sometimes called "5" for short).

Foot fault Called by a line judge when the server steps over the baseline before impacting the ball; the serve would then be a fault.

Forehand A shot that is hit on your dominant side (generally with the palm of your hand facing the net).

Grand Slam Winning all four major tournaments (Australian Open, French Open, Wimbledon and the U.S. Open) within a single year.

Groundstroke A forehand or backhand stroke hit after the ball has bounced.

Hitting zone The forward distance your racket travels with the ball after impact.

I-formation A starting position used in doubles. The server and his or her partner line up, with the partner in the middle of the court, at the net, and the server serving from just to either side of the center mark.

ITF International Tennis Federation—the governing body of tennis worldwide.

Let The call made when a served ball touches the net then lands in the service box. The server is allowed to replay the serve. A let is also called if, during a point, an interruption, such as a stray ball rolling onto the court, is noticed.

Lob A ball that travels in a high arc over the net.

Long A ball that lands beyond the baseline.

Love Represents a zero in proper tennis scoring. The term is thought to originate from the French word for egg, "l'oeuf," because an egg is shaped like a zero.

Lucky loser A player who loses in a qualifying tournament, but is entered into the main draw because of an unexpected vacancy. The lucky loser would have had the highest ranking of all the other losing players in the qualifier.

Match point The point before the end of the match, where if the player in the lead wins the next point he or she will win the match.

Net The middle divider of the tennis court, usually made of woven nylon, although sometimes metal fencing is used.

Open A tournament that is open to both professional and amateur players.

Passing shot A shot (usually a groundstroke) that is hit past your opponent when your opponent is at the net.

Poaching In doubles, the term used to describe the action of the server's partner crossing in front of the server to attack the return of serve at the net.

Professional A player who plays in tournaments that award prize money, or someone who earns money by giving tennis lessons.

Pusher A player who keeps getting the ball over the net with a soft shot, hoping for the opponent to make a mistake.

Qualifier A player who succeeds in earning a spot in the main draw of a tournament by winning a certain number of matches in a qualifying tournament.

Rally A series of continuous shots over the net.

Rankings The numerical order of players from best to worst in terms of their match wins.

Seeds The top players in a tournament are sometimes "seeded" and then split up in the draw so they will not meet up until later rounds (so the top players don't knock each other out of the tournament in the early rounds).

Serve The shot that starts each point in tennis. Also called "service."

Service Box There are two service boxes. Each is bounded by the net, the singles sideline, the service line and the center line. They encompass the area of the court in which the serve must bounce before the ball is considered in play.

Set A scoring term used to describe a portion of a tennis match. Most matches are the best two out of three sets; some are the best three out of five. A set usually calls for one player to win six games by a margin of two games.

Set point The point before the winning point of a set. A player with set point will win the set if he or she wins the next point.

Short A ball that lands between the net and the service line.

Singles sticks The sticks that are used on a doubles court to prop up the net for singles matches, to ensure that the net is 3 feet 6 inches (106 cm) high at the singles sidelines.

Skunk Means the same as bagel, except you can't eat it!

Sphairistike The name given to an early version of tennis, designed by Major Wingfield; comes from the Greek word for "play."

"T" The name of the area of each service box right beside the intersection of the service line and the center service line.

Tiebreaker A scoring system used to determine a winner of a set that has become tied at six games all.

Unforced error A point that is lost through the player's own fault, not because his opponent hit a winner.

Volley A ball that is hit out of the air.

Wild card A player who is given a spot in a tournament even though he or she failed to qualify (usually used for a formerly high-ranked player who is just coming off an injury, for a player who will attract more spectators to the tournament or to give a local, talented player a chance to compete).

Wimbledon A Grand Slam tournament, named for the area of London, England, where the British Open is held.

Tennis Resources

International Tennis Federation
Bank Lane, Roehampton
London, England SW1555XZ
Tel: (44) 208-878-6464
www.itftennis.com

International Wheelchair Tennis Association
Rue de Talus 112
F92500 Rueil
Malmaison, France
Tel: (331) 475-20108

Tennis Canada
3111 Steeles Avenue West
Downsview, Ontario
Canada M3J 3H2
Tel: (416) 665-9777
www.tenniscanada.com—has links to newsletters, provincial associations, wheelchair tennis and find-a-pro service

United States Tennis Association
70 West Red Oak Lane
White Plains, New York
U.S.A. 10604
Tel: (914) 696-7000
www.usta.com—tennis news, tournament news, rules, games, kids' zone, U.S. Open tickets

United States Professional Tennis Association
3535 Briarpark Drive,
Suite One
Houston, Texas
U.S.A. 77042
Tel: 1-800-USPTA-4U
www.uspta.com—find a pro, teaching tips, playing tips

Some more great tennis Web sites:

www.juniortennis.com—international junior information, rankings, player information, nutrition and fitness articles

www.tennisone.com—some great instructional video clips, as well as general tennis news

www.acemantennis.com—great site for checking up on women's tennis results anywhere in the world

www.wtatour.com—gives on and off court news about professional female players, tour results, coaches' tips

www.atptour.com—up-to-the-minute men's professional tour information

Index

Italicized numbers indicate illustrations

A
ace, 107
advantage, 107
Agassi, André, *89*
aggressive baseliner, 74, 75–77
All England Croquet Club, 14–15
all-white clothing rule, 23
alley, 107
amateurs, 15, 107
anticipation, 43–44, *46*
attacking the net, 82, 83–84
Australian Open, 101

B
backhand, 50–52, 107
backhand drills, 35–36, 53–54
bagel, 107
ball clip, 24
ball drills
  balancing on racket, 30, *30*
  high balls, 38
  keeping ball in air (volleying), 33–34
  receiving ball from ready position, 37–38
  rolling practice, 31, *31*
balls, 22–23
baseline, 43–45
bobble the ball, 85
Borg, Bjorn, 72
break point, 107
breaks, 107
breathing, 105
British Open. *See* Wimbledon
bye, 101, 107

C
Capriati, Jennifer, *72–73*
center of percussion, 21
chip and charge, 77
choice of server and receiver, 90
clothes, 23–24
Code of Conduct, 96–97, 107
Continental grip, 47, *47*, 50
continuous cycle of movement, *46*
court tennis, 14
courts
  doubles, 92
  lines, *24, 25*
  measurements, *24*, 25
  shape of, 14, 15
  surfaces, 17, 23
cross-court, 107

D
Davenport, Lindsay, *98–99*
Davis, Dwight, 101
Davis Cup, 75, 101, *101*, 107
defensive baseliner, 74, 75
dehydration, 106, 107
deuce, 107
digestion times, 104–105
Dokic, Jelena, *13*
dominant hand, 29, 30
double fault, 90
doubles
  attacking the net, 82, 83–84
  both players back, 82, 84
  communication, 85
  one up and one back, 82, 84
  rules, 92–93
  serve and volley, 60
  strategies, 82
  tactics, 83–85
  tiebreakers, 93
  traditional starting position, 60
down the line, 107
draw, 101, 107
drills
  backhand, 53–54
  ball drills. *See* ball drills
  catch and throw drill, 42
  centering drill, 53
  consistency drill, 43
  forehand, 53–54
  high/low drill, 45
  match the arc, 53
  practice drills. *See* practice drills
  receiving drill, 53
  right/left drill, 45
  service drills, 57–58
  shot drills, 52–53
  specialty shots. *See* specialty shot drills
  volley, 60–61
  warm-up. *See* warm-ups
  "yes" drill, 45
drive and charge, 77
drop, 107
Dwight, James, 15

E
Eastern backhand grip, 50
Eastern grip, *46*, 46–47
equipment
  balls, 22–23
  clothes, 23–24
  rackets, 20–21
  shoes, 23
etiquette, 94–97

F
faking, 83, 107
fault, 90–91, 108
Federation Cup, 101, 108
fifteen ("5"), 108
follow-through, 48
foot fault, 90–91, *91*, 108
forehand, 46–49, 107
French Open, 101

G
getting to the ball, 45
glossary of tennis terms, 107–109
Grand Slam, 101, 108
graphite rackets, 20
grips
  backhand, 50
  Continental grip, 47, *47*, 50
  Eastern backhand grip, 50
  Eastern grip, *46*, 46–47
  forehand grips, 46–47
  left-handed players, 47
  relaxed grip, 47
  Semi-western grip, 47, *47*
  serve, 56
  "shake hands" grip, *46*, 46–47
  two-handed backhand grip, 50
  volley, 60
groundstrokes
  backhand, 50–52
  forehand, 46–49
  meaning of, 108
gut, 21

H
Hewitt, Lleyton, *26–27*
Hingis, Martina, *80–81, 98–99*
hitting "into/out of the house," 78
hitting the ball. *See* shots
hitting zone, 48, *49*, 52, 108

I
I-formation, 83, 108
impact point, 66
International Tennis Federation (ITF), 17, 108

J
le jeu de paume, 14
junior rackets, 20

K
Knowles, Mark, 83, *83*
Kournikova, Anna, *40–41*

L
lawn tennis, 14–15
legs, use of, 33
let, 90, 96, 108
lines, *24, 25*
lob, 53, 64, 108
long, 108
love, 108
lucky loser, 108

M
match point, 108
McEnroe, John, 75
mini-tennis, 42–43
moon balls, 52

N
Navratilova, Martina, *19, 94–95*
Nestor, Daniel, 83, *83*
net rusher, 74, 77–79
nets, 25, 108
no advantage scoring, 89
nutrition, 104–105

O
open, 108
open stance, 48, 51
overhead smash, 64–66

P
passing shot, 108
patterns of play, 75–77
Pierce, Mary, *80–81, 102*
playing the game
  at the baseline, 43–45
  getting to the ball, 45
  hitting the ball. *See* shots
  mini-tennis, 42–43
poaching, 83, 108
pockets, 24
positions
  doubles, 60
  open stance, 48, 51
  ready position, *36*, 36–37, 39
  semi-open stance, 48, 51
  serves, 56
  square stance, 48, *49*, 50–51
practice drills
  backhand, 35–36
  catching frogs (drill), 31–33, *32*
  high balls, 38

hit the wall, 34–35
keeping ball in air (volleying), 33–34
racquet drills, 29–30
rallying with the wall, 38
rallying with yourself, 33
ready position, 36–37
receiving ball from ready position, 37–38
rolling the ball, 31, *31*
volleying against the wall, 38
warm-ups, 28–29
professionals, 15–16, 108
pusher, 109

Q
qualifier, 109

R
racket drills, 29–31
rackets
center of percussion, 21
described, 20, *21*
face, 107
strings, 21
sweet spot, 21
Rafter, Patrick, *11*, 59
rally balls, 52
rallying
hitting "into/out of the house," 78
meaning of, 33, 109
rally for consistency, 53
rally in the alley, 53
rally with targets, 54
strike zone, receiving ball in, 34
with the wall, 38
with yourself, 33
rankings, 109
ready position, *36*, 36–37, 39
receiving, rules of, 92
recovery, 51
Roddick, Andy, 59
rules
breaks, 92
choice of server and receiver, 90
double fault, 90
doubles, 92–93
foot fault, 90–91, *91*
no advantage scoring, 89
receiving, 92
scoring, 88–89
serving, 54, 90–91
tiebreakers, 88–89
time outs, 92

S
Sampras, Pete, 59
scoring, 88–89
seeds, 101, 109
Seles, Monica, *86–87*
semi-open stance, 48, 51
Semi-western grip, 47, *47*
serve and volley, 60
serves
adding spin, 58
advanced serve, *56*, 56–57
after tiebreakers, 88
described, 54–55
getting set to serve, 55–56
grip, 56
meaning of, 109
rules, 90–91
slice serves, 58
topspin serve, 58
service box, 109
service breaks, 107
service drills
impact drill, 58
serving wide, 77
tossing drill, 57
two-ball drill, 57–58
service return, 74
set, 109
set point, 109
"shake hands" grip, *46*, 46–47
shoes, 23
short, 109
shot drills
drive, 52
lob, 53
moon balls, 52
rally balls, 52
topspin dipper, 53
shots
backhand, 50–52
forehand, 46–49
groundstrokes, 46–54
the serve, 54–58
sidespin, 49
specialty shots. *See* specialty shots
topspin, 49
underspin, 49
volley, 58–61
sidespin, 49
singles sticks, 109
skunk, 109
slice serves, 58
specialty shot drills
drop shot progression drill, 67–69
lob drill, 64
lob/overhead drill, 66
overhead progression drill, 66
pick-up ball drills, 70–71
specialty shots, 64–66
Sphairistike, 14, *15*, 109
spins, 58
square stance, 48, *49*, 50–51
stances. *See* positions
strategies
aggressive baseliner, 74
defensive baseliner, 74
doubles, 82
net rusher, 74
strike zone
described, 31, *32*
positioning, 37
receiving in, 34, *44*
strings, 21
strokes. *See* shots
Summer Olympics, 12
sweet spot, 21

T
"T," 77, 109
tactics
aggressive baseliner tactics, 75–77
defensive baseliner tactics, 75
doubles, 83–85
net rusher tactics, 77–79
sophisticated, 83
tennis
earnings, 16, 93
history of, 14–16
longest match, 75
origins of, 14
resources, 110
tiebreakers, 88–89, 93, 109
time outs, 92
topspin, 49
topspin dipper, 53
topspin serve, 58
touching the net, 84, 91
tournaments
balls, use of, 22
bye, 101, 107
competition levels, 101
described, 98
draw, 101, 107
draw sheet (sample), *100*
"Grand Slam," 101
professionals, 16
seeds, 101, 109
wild card, 101
two-handed backhand grip, 50

U
underspin, 49
unforced error, 109
unit turn, 37, *48*
U.S. Open, 101

V
Vicario, Arantxa Sanchez, *18*, *94–95*
volley
described, 59–60
in doubles, 60
grip, 60
meaning of, 109
serve and volley, 60
volley drills
baseline volley, 61
reflex volley drill, 60–61
volley game, 61
warm-up, 33–34

W
wall drills, 34–35, 38
warm-ups
ankle rolls, 28, *28*
high knees, 29, *29*
jumping over line, 28, *28*
running on the spot, 28
skipping, *28*
upper body, 29, *29*
wrist rolls, 28, *28*
water, 106
wheelchair athletes, *17*
Wilander, Mats, 75
wild card, 101, 109
Williams, Serena, *16*, 59, *62–63*
Wimbledon, 15, 101, 109
Wingfield, Walter Clopton, 14